Contemporary Chinese Theatre

Contemporary Chinese Theatre

Roger Howard

Heinemann London Hong Kong Singapore Kuala Lumpur

HEINEMANN EDUCATIONAL BOOKS (ASIA) LTD
Yik Yin Building, 321-323 To Kwa Wan Road, Kowloon, Hong Kong
41 Jalan Pemimpin, Singapore 20
Suite 4012-4013, The Regent, Jalan Imbi, Kuala Lumpur 06-23, Malaysia

Heinemann Educational Books Ltd
48 Charles Street, London W1X 8AH, England
Associated companies, branches & representatives throughout the world

ISBN 0 435 18456 3

First published 1978

Set in 11 point Garamond
by Graphicraft Typesetters
and printed in Hong Kong by
New Kowk Hing Printing Press Co., Ltd

Contents

Preface

This book arose out of articles in *Theatre Quarterly* (Vol. 1 No. 4 and Vol. 2 No. 8). I would like to thank the editors and publishers of that journal for the use of a part of the articles in the present work.

China's contemporary drama is intimately linked with her people's struggle for modernization. A high proportion of her new plays deal with problems of economic, and particularly agricultural, development. These plays set all developing countries an example of a dramatic culture expressing, and to some extent propelling, economic, social and political regeneration after centuries of feudal exploitation and, latterly, imperialist interference.

This book has not, of course, been able to present more than a sketch of this broad and turbulent background to the new drama it describes. Fortunately, there are a number of serious studies of the Chinese revolution available now and the reader might be helped in his understanding of the drama if he used the present book alongside a more general history. A brief chronology of events has, however, been included here.

Brief Chronology

1911	Revolution. End of the Ch'ing dynasty. Republic declared
1919	May Fourth Movement
1921	Founding of the Chinese Communist Party (C.C.P.)
1924—27	First Revolutionary Civil War: Kuomintang (K.M.T.) and C.C.P. against warlords
1926	Communist-led peasant associations in south China
1927	Chiang Kai-shek turns against C.C.P.: thousands executed
1927—35	Second Revolutionary Civil War: C.C.P. against K.M.T.
1928	Mao Tse-tung and Chu Teh set up red base in Chingkang Mountains. Founding of Workers' and Peasants' Revolutionary Army
1929—34	Kiangsi Soviet
1935	Long March
1936	United Front between C.C.P. and K.M.T.
1936—47	Yenan base
1937—45	War of Resistance against Japan
1942	Mao's *Talks at the Yenan Forum on Literature and Art*
1946—49	War of Liberation (against K.M.T.). Land reform
1949	(October) Founding of the People's Republic
1950—53	Korean War
1955	Acceleration of agricultural cooperative movement
1956—57	Hundred Flowers Movement
1957	Mao's *On the Correct Handling of Contradictions among the People*
1958—59	Great Leap Forward and the communes
1960	Russian advisers withdrawn
1965—70	Great Proletarian Cultural Revolution
1971	Lin Piao's conspiracy and death
1974	Movement to repudiate Lin Piao and Confucius
1976	Death of Mao. Overthrow of Chiang Ch'ing

Part One

CHAPTER ONE

Historical Background

Performing arts existed in China at the time of the first dynasties 4,000 years ago but their nature is uncertain. In the Chou dynasty (1122—221 B.C.) they consisted mainly of spiritualistic ceremonies and temple dances played at religious festivals. Palace entertainment was provided by dancers and singers and court jesting by dwarfs and clowns. Thus at that pre-feudal period the use of theatrical art as an expression of class rule was already established.

By the end of the slave society and the beginning of the classical feudal period under China's unifier, Emperor Ch'in Shih Huang, in the third century B.C., performances had hardly developed beyond the stage of dances and impromptu acting. However, acrobatics reached China about this time, probably from central Asia, and shadow plays are thought to have originated in the reign of Emperor Wu Ti (140—87 B.C.). Puppet plays began to be shown about 200 years later. In the T'ang dynasty (A.D. 618—907) the imperial court set up a school to train girls to dance, sing poems and play music. Short satirical and dramatic plays began to develop from dances and skits.

With the growth of the landlord and tenant system, the building of cities under the T'ang and the increased importance of the great wealthy families or clans, distinct from the court, the Sung dynasty (A.D. 960—1279) saw the extension of theatrical entertainment to wider groups within the educated classes and to a certain extent outside, though play writing was scorned by the scholar officials as a vulgar activity. Theatres were built in the towns and cities. Professional and amateur actors performed dramas that told simple stories with the help of dancing, music and acrobatics. Guilds, or groups, of professional writers provided scripts of plays, stories and songs, aided by ballad forms of poetry that became more highly developed under the Sung. Plays shown on temporary stages in the streets were an important part of the religious festivals celebrated according to the lunar calendar. The scope of plays at court banquets and other imperial festivities was broad: historical, military, literary, supernatural, romantic, moralistic, satirical, farcical and realistic stories no doubt gave these dramas their name of *tsa chu*, or variety plays.

At this time shadow and puppet plays attained great heights of development and influenced the styles of movement and gesture used by actors in the flesh-and-blood dramas.

A type of poetic drama, telling a story in songs and dialogue and using more colloquial language and popular tunes, developed around the city of Hangchow and became known as Southern Drama. But these plays were soon overshadowed by the great dramatic development which took place in northern China in the Yüan dynasty (1234/1280—1368), the richest period of dramatic literature China has known.

In the Yüan, China was ruled by Mongol conquerors whom the Chinese literati regarded as uncivilized but who nevertheless appreciated drama, music and songs. More important, the Mongols broke the monopoly that the Confucian scholars had on the arts. The scholars, forced to make a living, dropped their disdain for drama and took up writing plays to make money. Previously they could have expected high official rank and they used plays to express their resentment at being forced into mundane obscurity. They showed their opposition to alien rule by writing plays of romantic escapism into the religious and supernatural and, more directly, through dramas of lives blighted by corruption and oppression. Other playwrights, closer to the people, wrote dramas about heroic brigands, such as those of Shantung province who feature in the well-known story *Water Margin*, who sallied from their mountain strongholds to help the poor and oppressed and rob the rich. Their wealth of characters, incident and subject matter and their technical soundness made the Yüan plays outstanding.

In the Ming dynasty (1368—1644) the softer southern school superseded the more military northern school. In the sixteenth century Soochow became the centre of a poetic style of drama, *kunchü*, which remained the dominant form until the nineteenth century. Scholars once more sought rank among the official class and the language of drama became more literary, losing much of the colloquial and dramatic quality it had had under the Yüan. Playwrights concentrated on historical and literary themes and paid little attention in their work to contemporary or social affairs. The writing of drama became a literary pastime.

With the continuing influence of the great clans and their stress on ancestral sacrifices came the practice of holding theatrical performances to accompany the rites in the ancestral temples of the landlord and official families. The custom was extended to performing dramas at other family ceremonies, from the taking of a bride to the death of a relation. Besides these public or semi-public performances, private shows were given, especially at banquets of the scholars. *Kunchü* was popular with the scholars and in the trading cities rich merchants also patronized it.

Cruder forms of drama, associated with the peasants' sacrifices to the gods of the harvest, were played in the villages. Every village had a temple where performances took place during festivals, often as part of temple fairs and usually in the winter months. Through these dramas of tribute and worship, the peasants, encouraged by monks, thanked the gods for the last harvest and prayed for the next one. Other dramatic offerings were made at the lunar new year, before or around sowing time. Secret societies used these gatherings, which attracted huge crowds, as covers for meetings; and the government of the Ch'ing (Manchu) dynasty (1644—1911), especially in the late eighteenth and early nineteenth century, being worried about the gradual breakdown of the imperial system, tried to restrict the peasants' performances, either censoring them or forbidding them. The ethical basis of the dramas themselves, however, whether religious or secular, was largely Confucian, and as such served the interests of the feudal rulers well enough.

The temple plays were supplemented in north China by *yangko* dances, originally rice-transplanting songs. As late as 1926 Sydney Gamble found thirty-six *yangko* groups performing village plays and dances in one county of Hopei province alone, with a population of about 400,000. Most of the *yangko* plays were likewise connected with the worship of gods, while those on everyday themes, such as love and family relations, depicted life, according to Gamble, 'as represented by high society' rather than the reality the peasants knew. Apart from *yangko*, there were processions at festival times of bearers carrying a painted dragon lit by lanterns. Troupes of acrobats and performers of the military arts of *wushu* called at the villages, bringing with them the lion dance, familiar today as an item in the programme of Chinese acrobatic companies on their tours abroad.

As a reaction by the scholars and officials of the capital against the domination of a local drama in soft southern style, a northern school, *chingchu*, or Peking drama — what we know as Peking opera

— emerged in the nineteenth century. It was based on tunes imported from Anhwei in the south but it mixed in with them tunes from the north and north-west. The new school continued to depict historical and literary heroes and heroines of the declining feudal rulers. Few new plays were written and the best known artists were not playwrights but actors, famous primarily for their singing. What distinguished the Peking opera from the *kunchü* was its style of music and the acting and production conventions it developed and rigidly observed — the song styles, gestures, movements, painted faces and costumes for which the Peking school became known throughout the world. While the acting conventions were strict, the range was broad. The Peking style embraced the acrobatics and tumbling of the heroes of stories of the supernatural, the boisterous sword fights of the generals, the languid indolent grace of the court ladies and the sedate dignity of the officials and scholars.

The Peking theatre received patronage from the courts of the last emperors of China as well as from the rich officials and landlords. But performances were held not only at court or in private houses but also in the city's theatre-restaurants and tea-houses. After the overthrow of the Ch'ing dynasty in 1911 when they could no longer be retained by the court, many actors turned professional and formed their own troupes using the tea-houses as company bases.

From the time of the 1911 revolution Chinese cultural reformers increasingly demanded a modern theatre capable of expressing the feelings and aspirations of a new China. They found their own drama hidebound by theatrical and thematic tradition. They regarded it at first as largely superfluous and turned instead to writing in foreign styles. After attempts in the years 1907—19 to write romantic and symbolist dramas with an uneasy combination of old and new techniques, young writers under the influence of the May Fourth Movement of 1919 adopted naturalism and realism and these have formed the basis of *huachu* (modern spoken drama, distinct from opera) until the present time. Ibsen, Shaw and Chekhov were the western playwrights most seriously studied.

In the early 1920s the modern drama made little headway. In 1924—27 a number of amateur dramatic societies put on plays with sharp social messages condemning the feudal marriage system, the rule of the warlords and the oppression of the workers. In 1928 the leftist bourgeois playwright Tien Han set up a dramatic club, the

South China Society, which took plays on social themes on tours of southern cities. The club was suppressed by the Kuomintang (Nationalist) government in 1930. Meanwhile the well-known actor of women's roles, Mei Lan-fang, scored successes in the traditional Peking opera by writing a series of new plays, 'ancient costume dramas', based on old plots, tunes and dance forms. These were well received by theatre audiences at home and on tour in Japan, the United States and the Soviet Union.

But the most significant development was taking place, not in the cities among the progressive intelligentsia and still less among devotees of Peking opera, but among the peasants of the south China mountains. In 1928 workers', peasants' and soldiers' dramatic troupes were formed in Kiangsi province, as the Fourth Red Army of Mao Tse-tung and General Chu Teh began a revolutionary land reform there. Red Army propaganda units used short agitational plays to rouse the peasants to throw off the 2,000-year-old feudal rule of the landlords. By 1931 sixty troupes had been organized to tour the local villages.

Thus, while bourgeois intellectuals of the cities developed a westernized, theatre-based drama of social conscience, the Red Army was taking the traditional ballad and dance forms of the countryside and turning them into agitational plays for revolutionary use in the awakening villages. They gained the support of peasants, who gave food and lodging and provided transport. The Red units continued to use drama as 'a seeding-machine', as Mao put it, of new revolutionary ideas during the Long March westwards. The custom deepened and spread when in 1936 Mao's armies reached the Yenan area of northern Shensi and set up a base there from which to fight the Japanese in north China and, later, the Kuomintang.

During the anti-Japanese war of 1937—45, patriotic drama groups in the Kuomintang-controlled areas toured cities and country towns putting over the idea that the war was mainly one of national defence against the invaders. The communists in Yenan, on the other hand, used drama, including *yangko* dances and plays, to convey a class-based message that the war was mainly a mass revolutionary struggle.

After the Japanese defeat, the communist drama groups developed the use of agitational drama in the new war against the Kuomintang. They turned *yangko* from a superstitious rice-transplanting song and dance into a highly effective weapon against the landlords and their Kuomintang backers, vigorous, often satirical and moreover Chinese — 'struggle *yangko*', as the peasants called them — while they developed the *yangko* plays into equally popular operas on land reform themes.

Among the leftist city dramatists in the Kuomintang-controlled areas there was a feeling of isolation. Their social conscience plays exposed the nature of Kuomintang rule — dependence on international big business, corruption, terror and landlord tyranny over the peasants — and thus helped to weaken it, but the writers stopped short of 'merging with the masses', as Mao Tse-tung urged intellectuals to do in his *Talks at the Yenan Forum on Literature and Art* in 1942. Progressive playwrights such as Tien Han, Hsia Yen and Tsao Yu had broken the conventions imposed by the traditional Chinese forms of drama and were striving to make foreign forms national and popular. Yet many of them began to feel that to discard the old operas was to ignore the fact that among the people the traditional styles were still loved while the unfamiliar modern drama in the western style was difficult for the masses, especially the peasants, to accept.

In Yenan the policy was to embark on a gradual transformation of the *yangko* and the old operas. The Yenan Peking Opera Company produced a story of peasant suffering and uprising, *Driven to Join the Liang Mountain Rebels*, which Mao praised as 'restoring historical truth' since it showed peasants, and not princes, as heroes. He said it 'opened up a new life for the old opera.'[1] The *yangko* dramas *Brothers and Sisters Open up Wasteland* and *The White-haired Girl* were produced by the Lu Hsun Academy in Yenan. These musical plays owed something to the modern drama (*huachu*) — in particular in their more realistic approach to dialogue, costume and acting — and they in turn later influenced the Peking opera.

The question of where to set the meeting-point of foreign and Chinese culture has been at the background of all China's development of the past 130 years. How much should modern western-style drama spread and how 'Chinese' should it become? How much should Chinese dance absorb the influence of western ballet? Drama workers both inside and outside the Chinese Communist Party have differed over these issues. But the deepest division in the Chinese theatre since 1928 has been over the question of what form propaganda should take — realism and naturalism and the drama of social conscience on the one hand, or agitational plays based on rural forms on the

Above: *Seminal drama in Yenan, 1945:* The White-haired Girl, *musical drama by the Lu Hsun Academy. Hsi-erh exposes the landlord, 'Let vengeance be done.'* (pp. 8, 33, 52, 64, 81)

ght: *Balancing act: Liu ing-yang, of the Shang- i Acrobatic Company, es a flower between her eth while spinning ites.* (pp. 14, 25, 37)

other. Linked to that is the even more complex question of the traditional opera, which is open to influence from either direction. At the bottom of these problems lie differences in political attitude among theatre artists.

Thus in 1949, when the Communist Party took power in China, the seeds of future conflict over drama were already sown. With the war won, the cultural cadres of the Party — now leading the country from the cities instead of fighting in the villages — would have to supervise a transformation of urban as well as rural drama. At first their common aim was to establish a revolutionary, modern, proletarian drama which was also national and reflected Chinese traditions. But they differed over means, and in settling the question of means they began to differ over aims. The next twenty-five years saw the gradual weakening of social conscience drama and the emergence during the cultural revolution of a strengthened agitational drama and a revolutionized Peking opera, with equivalent changes in the other theatre arts. Yet the question is not settled. The emerging forms have been widely challenged. China's feudal culture lasted several thousand years. Her new culture is perhaps twenty-five, at the most seventy, years old. The struggle to forge a drama reflecting and aiding the transformation and modernization of Chinese society has only just begun.

CHAPTER TWO

The Forms of Theatre

Peking Opera

Peking drama is customarily called opera in the west but it has little resemblance to European opera. In common with all traditional Asian theatre, it sets out to create patterns of sound and movement. In the Chinese theatre these patterns derive from the language. In spoken Chinese each word is given one of four tones. The rising, falling or level intonation of a word gives the word its meaning, and the same sound intoned in two, three or four different ways may make two, three or four quite different words.

From early times the tonal movement in the spoken language gave the writer of songs the basis for his composition. Music and language were thus integrated in a tonal relationship of great importance for Chinese opera. The sounds emitted by the singing voice in Peking opera today are no more and no less than one element in an aural and visual pattern created by the music (played by the orchestra) and the movement (created by the actors' gesture, mime and dance).

The Chinese opera-goer, like his western counterpart, goes to hear the singing and the music. But he also goes as a witness of a total performance. He delights in watching performers (including musicians, who traditionally sat on stage) play out a relationship between voice, music, gesture, mime and dance. The establishing of this relationship exercises the greatest skill of the performers. The actor has to submit to a line of sound and a line of movement, both of which travel continuously throughout the play. The musician, commenting on, reinforcing and sometimes contradicting the words, makes an organic contribution to the verbal expression. A song will be applauded by the audience not primarily for its particular expression, its passion or restraint, but for the way the actor indicates and confirms, through voice and gesture, the relationship of the particular song to the organic whole. The audience applauds the actor's success in merging with, and not standing out from, the whole.

This domination of formal qualities over expressive qualities gave the old Peking opera both its refined elegance and its conventional conservatism. Once an actor had perfected a gesture representing a certain action or emotion, there seemed little reason to try another. If at a point in a play a famous actor had made a certain movement, that movement would often become a part of future performances of the role by later actors. Complicated stage business was handed down from master to trainee. Indeed, the techniques became too difficult for anyone but the highly-trained to attempt.

Once they had learnt the intricacies of the form, however, the more outstanding and imaginative actors, such as Tan Hsin-pei and Mei Lan-fang, did embellish on what was handed down and develop their own characteristics. But since actors generally constructed a performance around a basic plot, taken from history, by pulling together scenes from existing plays, they acted within a tradition in which every type of character, every manner of entry and exit and every mood had already been set by dramatic convention. Thus the actor's opportunity for innovation was limited and even original contributions of the most individual actors sometimes amounted to no more than the unique finesse with which he or she mimed a conventional action — riding a horse, stepping over a threshold or hiding a laugh with the sleeve of a robe.

Musicians and playwrights faced similar limitations. The two principle musical modes found in Peking opera, *hsi-pi* and *erh-huang*, used fixed and restricted rhythmic patterns to express mood. The same melody was repeated in play after play and the test of the musicians' and playwrights' skill was to place it successfully in the construction of a new or rearranged plot according to the mood required. Even today, after Peking opera has been revolutionized, audiences applaud a passage sung to a familiar melody when they recognize how well the old tune has been fitted into the new setting.

The interest an audience takes in an actor's performance is largely restricted to an appreciation of technical virtuosity, the ability of the actor to depict a role within the conventions laid down for it. A.C. Scott's judgement that the Peking opera actor 'does not create individual characters so much as personality types' representing 'abstractions of human attributes' is as true of modern revolutionary opera as of the old feudal opera.[2] The types are such that an audience can have little interest in the portrayal of character. The use of painted faces for some roles in the traditional opera and the keeping of stage sets and properties to a minimum emphasized the formalism. The abandonment of these features in modern revolutionary Peking opera and the recent use of more naturalistic dialogue only partly reduces the artificiality.

But the virtuosity of a leading Peking opera actor is certainly very considerable. He must be a superior singer, mime and dancer, as well as actor, and he must have acquired the military arts of sword play, tumbling, somersaults and other acrobatics. His body must be superlatively fit, a high-precision instrument for carrying out complex patterns of aural and visual movement.

The minimum use of naturalism and realism in creating roles, the reliance on mime, and the conception of the stage as an area of space in which to shape abstract patterns, made Peking opera a suitable vehicle for moral didacticism in feudal China. Peking opera after 1949 has been the main battleground in the struggle to use theatre to spread the new morality and the didactic function of this old art has remained intact.

What has changed is the subject matter, the types of hero and, to some extent, the staging. Today, stories are realistic, the heroes are peasant and worker leaders and the staging is more natural. Women play women's roles. The music, based on old tunes, has been rewritten to suit the new hero-types. The singing remains shrill and most voices are constrained. The acting style while a singer sings is simpler and more direct. With the stress put on the heroic characters, there is less room for the bad and comic characters, with a consequent loss in variety of singing styles. Painted faces and splendid costumes have given way to more realistic make-up and everyday working clothes. The language of the dialogue, even when rhymed, has been brought closer to everyday speech, though the songs are still in a more traditional literary style and, since they are difficult for many to understand, their words are projected on to a screen at the side of the stage. Gestures and movements have less refinement and more boldness. Sets are realistic, colourful and even bulky. Forester's huts, peasant houses, wharfside buildings and mountain caves are brought on stage, reconstructed in careful detail, a major innovation compared with the sparse traditional background of perhaps a painted cloth. Lighting and special effects, with the help of back projections, underline the heroic feats — soldiers swing on trailing vines over a gorge and climb a mountain in a snowstorm, peasants link arms to hold back a river with the weight of their bodies and a partisan makes a getaway on an express locomotive in a cloud of steam. These scenes are backed by full sound effects of pelting rain, gale-force winds, rushing water and shrill whistles. The graceful Yang Kuei-fei, heroine of *The Drunken Concubine*, Mei Lan-fang's most popular role, no longer puts a wine-cup on a tray by bending over backwards and placing it there with her teeth. Physical virtuosity in a more martial tradition is expected of the actors and the old plays about famous generals of ancient times have their parallel in the new operas praising the exploits of the People's Liberation Army (P.L.A.). The titles themselves indicate that the era of courtly sorrow, Taoist philosophizing and scholarly romance has receded before the swords and rifles of the peasants' and workers' army. *The Emperor's Farewell to His Favourite, The Butterfly Dream* and *Picking up the Jade Bracelet* have given place to *Raid on the White Tiger Regiment*, *Fighting on the Plains* and *Red Detachment of Women*.

The new revolutionary 'model' operas are normally played in full, but selected scenes are taught to amateur troupes. In November 1972 the 600-year-old practice of showing *chetzuhsi*, a programme made up of excerpts from a number of operas, was revived, but with a difference. Whereas formerly the scenes selected often related to each other and, slightly adapted, made up a whole new play, the 1972 programme was made up of six scenes from Peking operas and revolutionary ballets unrelated except in their revelation, according to *Peking Review*, of 'the rich expressive power of the modern Peking opera' and 'the successful application of ballet techniques to portray the struggle and life of the Chinese people.'[3]

Local Operas

The relationship between Peking opera and local operas is flexible and complex. What is now Peking opera started as a local opera but because of its location in the capital, its promotion by the court and its use of a dialect which, being spoken over wide areas of China, formed the basis of standard Chinese, it gradually assumed the character of a national form and it is as such that it is regarded today. But while it is the outstanding form of Chinese drama, it is still one from among many.

Between two and three hundred forms of local opera exist. Perhaps 100 of these are in use today. They differ from Peking opera in that traditionally they used local dialect, local music and their own styles of singing and acting. Since the cultural revolution the local forms have been much changed. Using the revolutionary Peking operas as models, frivolous and sentimental tunes have been cut out and languid music has been made more vigorous. Variety has been added by taking tunes from Peking opera and other local forms and from folk songs, and by varying the types of instruments used. The vocabulary of gestures and movements has been extended by borrowing further from traditional Chinese boxing and from folk dances and western ballet as well as from everyday life and work. Acrobatics have been introduced into certain local forms that had none.

Though the main task since 1970 has been to adapt the model Peking operas, local operas do not take from a model without giving in return. The policy for all drama companies is to 'learn from each other' in pursuing the twin objectives of 'popularizing' complex artistic forms and 'raising the cultural level' of workers and peasants so they can appreciate them better. Thus there is a great deal of borrowing in line with the traditional view of a play's text as something far from static but rather a source which can be divided up and reused. Tunes from local operas are used in *Song of the Dragon River* and *Red Detachment of Women*, thus enlarging the musical expression of Peking opera. *Shachiapang* was adapted from a local Shanghai opera into a Peking opera, became a model and then, in the process of being 'popularized' as a model Peking opera, spread over the country. It was promoted by the 'model book' of the text, by study classes and courses, by festival and tour performances, by a film of the stage version and by performances of local Peking opera companies, until finally it was re-adapted into a great many local opera forms. This two-way, down-up, up-down process of adaptation is typical of play writing since the cultural revolution. The regions make the experiments, Peking checks up on them and adopts a few which it then turns into models for the regions to copy and multiply.

The great majority of local operas, however, are not transformed into Peking operas and do not become models. Most reach only the stage of commendation by the central authorities, being submitted for inspection and criticism at the provincial and national festivals. Local drama workers, as well as local political pressure groups within the Communist Party, make their opinions known, using these occasions as their setting and the operas as their means. Commendation is by no means automatic. Even those operas that are approved will be treated to extensive criticism, verbally after public and private shows, and later in the press, when revisions will be suggested both by cultural officials and by workers, peasants and soldiers. Local troupes also face the possibility of disfavour. The Shansi Opera Company's production of *Three Ascents of Peach Mountain*, written collectively by the Writing Group of the Cultural Bureau of Shansi province and shown at the North China Drama Festival in Peking in January 1974, was taken off after one performance and condemned in the press as 'a very poisonous weed'. It was said to have pleaded the case of a number of political leaders who had fallen from power during the cultural revolution.

Even with the stylistic changes of recent years, local operas retain many distinctive features. These are a mixture of the traditional and the new.

Pingchu, found in north and central China, grew out of the peasant ballads of Hopei province during the past seventy years. It is lively and down-to-earth, its songs are in standard speech and easy to understand, and the singing style is today robust and unconstrained. A *pingchu* troupe in Liaoning province recently experimented with the use of some ballet techniques in their adaptations of model Peking operas.

Cantonese *yuehchu* from Kwangtung province in the south has a less rigid singing style than Peking opera, is less shrill, more evocative and until recently could also be counted as soft and delicate. The 1973 film of *Shachiapang* in this local form reveals that the style is bolder and louder today.

Kunchü, originating in the Ming dynasty, uses a soft flute as the leading instrument to blend with the poetical dialogue. Movements are even more closely integrated with the singing than in Peking opera. The actor dances and moves continuously while he sings.

Pangtzu, a northern form, exists in two types, one from Hopei and one from Shansi province. The name comes from *pangtzu*, a block of wood beaten with a wooden stick which originally was used by Buddhist monks chanting the sacred texts. This custom gave rise to its secular use in local ballads and it is used today to beat time for the orchestra. Its clicking sound is a distinctive feature of this opera form. The singing style is richer and more forceful than that of Peking opera. Instead of coming from the throat, the voice comes mainly from the chest and the sound is less constrained.

Yuehchu, a form of Shaohsing opera, was generally played by women from sometime after its founding in Shaohsing, near Hangchow in the south, about ninety years ago. The cultural revolution finally put a stop to this custom and both actors and actresses appear in the revised form. The music is strident, though softer than Peking opera, and the singing is natural. Movements are fluid and graceful. It has traditionally had realistic scenery but amateur peasant *yuehchu* companies used little.

Szechuan opera, *chuanchu*, is melodious and poetical. The singer is accompanied only by percussion and he uses a natural voice. Sometimes he is backed by a small chorus of female voices who may narrate the story or join in with the singer. Some of these features have probably been modified by revision.

Huaku (flower drum) is a small-scale form from Hunan province which for nearly 200 years featured only three roles: a young man, a young woman and a clown. It has been revised to encompass larger themes than the romantic and domestic affairs which were previously its staple and tunes regarded as monotonous and sentimental have been given more vigour.

Modern Drama (huachu)

Modern drama derived from the west and developed in the Kuomintang-controlled cities in the 1920s and 1930s as social conscience drama and in the 1940s as a drama of national defence, a weapon in the anti-Japanese war. Major influences were Hauptmann and O'Neill but the patriotic war dramas also showed the influence of Russian realism. From 1950 to 1960 Russian advisers attached to the Central Dramatic Institute in Peking brought Chinese playwrights and actors into closer contact with Soviet ideas on socialist realism. The ideological base of the Stanislavsky Method — the 'self' as the repository of character — was rejected by radical drama workers in the cultural revolution, although formally and technically many features of the Method continue to be utilized today. Characterization is still stressed but the psychology of individuals is more and more related to social and class causes.

Actors have become less inclined to cultivate themselves as stars and a collective style of work has spread. More technical discipline has been learnt and a vocabulary of gestures and stage movements has been built up which, while it is influenced by Peking and local opera techniques, is less symbolic and more naturalistic.

Huachu (literally, 'speaking dramas') were formerly only really popular with the urban educated classes and the aim of the recent changes has been to give a national form to this import from abroad to make it more widely appreciated. The transformation of modern drama from a minority to a mass art is aided by its use of standard Chinese. If dialect is used it is usually the odd line containing a local saying or some verbal humour. Only a few play writing groups use dialect throughout. While modern dramas depict characters from different social classes all speaking standard Chinese, in real life workers in, for example, Peking, while keeping the same tones as other classes, use different pronunciation and even different vocabulary. Some local actors and playwrights reflect these differences, though they are not great. In areas where the local dialect is more extreme, such as in Shanghai and the south, the Chinese spoken on stage in *huachu* sounds very different from that spoken in the street. Officially the language of *huachu* is said to be 'a literary language deriving from the living language but more concise.'[4]

While Peking operas are divided into scenes, normally between seven and eleven, *huachu* follows the western tradition of division into acts. These are usually three, four or five in number. Some one-act plays, usually comedies, also derive from the modern drama tradition, though they take too from local opera styles and agitational plays.

Writers of modern dramas have in general to find out what the people like and resist imposing a foreign form indiscriminately on an uncomprehending audience. As familiarity with the form grows, more people have been accepting *huachu* and most provinces and cities and many large towns have permanent professional companies.

Agitational Sketches

The evolution of the agitational sketch shows that though their content changes rapidly with the times, the forms used today are much as they were forty years ago. Propaganda plays were first used by the Communist Party on an organized, though still local, scale in 1931, when the Gorky School in Juichin in the Kiangsi Soviet area in south China began to train theatrical troupes to tour the villages and propagate ideas of resistance and revolt as part of the war effort against the Kuomintang. Each Red Army and most departments of the communists' civil administration had its own troupe. On the Long March and in Yenan the troupes increased in number and influence.

During the anti-Japanese war much agitational drama subscribed not to the official Party slogan 'For a Literature of National Defence', which with Chou Yang as its leading spokesman was followed by the *huachu* writers under the terms of the United Front with the Kuomintang, but to the leftist slogan, evidently approved by Mao, of a rival group around the non-communist revolutionary writer Lu Hsun, 'For a Mass Literature for the National Revolutionary War'. The differences, which may not have been generally apparent in creative work at the time, are significant in retrospect. The question was whether to stress in the arts national or revolutionary interests, national defence or revolutionary war, city or rural leadership. It was these differences that remained unresolved after 1949 and indeed are still so today.

An agitational performance during the anti-Japanese war on an open-air stage in a village street, converted temple or school yard or on an army drill ground might consist of one-act dramas, *yangko* dances, news items, mime, folk-songs with new revolutionary words, stories and ballads. In 1938 in one performance given on a bare stage in a temple yard at the communist army headquarters in Shansi's Wutai Mountains, local players of the Eighth Route Army's troupe sang a ballad *The Battle of Pinghsing Pass* to soldiers who had just fought and won it, while a Shanghai troupe touring the front played a comic melodrama *On the Banks of the Whangpoo* about dockers' anti-Japanese resistance in Shanghai. When someone in the audience suggested to the visiting players that life in Shanghai was remote from the Shansi peasants, overnight the troupe came up with a new play *Defence of the Village*, in local dialect, about a peasant family resisting the invaders.[5]

A *yangko* show in Yenan in the early 1940s comprised a dance in which the spectators took part, a short play, followed by another dance, and so on, the whole lasting as long as three or four hours. The villains of the plays were Japanese soldiers, Chinese traitors, witch doctors and loafers who hampered the war effort. The heroes and heroines were Eighth Route Army soldiers, militiamen, and local political leaders struggling for mutual aid in the fight against superstition, illiteracy and disease, as well as model workers in villages, factories, cooperatives and government offices who had done good work for the war effort and for production. The whole show ended with a final dance and song summarizing the moral.[6]

An anti-illiteracy sketch of the period showed how an old peasant received a letter from his son in the local town saying that the price of beans had gone up. As he could not read, he showed the letter to a neighbour who told him it said the price of peas had gone up. It was nearly time to harvest the grain and if he left the fields he might lose his crop. Nevertheless, the peasant set off for the market with his peas. He cursed when he found the price of peas was not high at all and returned to the village where he found his son had already sold the beans, the grain was ruined and his daughter-in-law, who could read, was swearing at him for his illiteracy. Amid the audience's laughter, the old peasant resolved to 'wipe out my illiteracy'.[7]

Even Japanese prisoners-of-war formed a group which, in 1944 in Yenan, gave a programme of folk-songs such as *Disgusting Life in the Army* and *Anti-war March*, and a short play about a soldier defecting to the communists which ended with the actors stamping on their national flag.[8]

During the War of Liberation against the Kuomintang, agitational drama, largely sponsored by the People's Liberation Army, spread political and general education, stimulated land reform and agricultural production and raised the morale of the soldiers.

Today amateur propaganda teams attached to factories, communes, army units, offices, universities and most workplaces of any size perform short sketches using songs and dances, gestures and mime to propagate either a general or a particular political idea invariably related to the needs of current mass movements and ideological campaigns. Performed in the open street or commune yard or in a factory auditorium, village hall or similar meeting place, but rarely in theatres, they employ charm, vigour, colour and sometimes satire to convey their message, perhaps encapsulated in a sung slogan at the end or in a slogan inscribed in white or yellow on a red banner held or hung behind the performers. In the cultural revolution, Red Guard groups made much use of Mao's portrait in their items, marching behind it and wheeling to kneel in front of it with hands outstretched and backs to the audience, the portrait's the only face visible. But this has declined. The actors dress either in their everyday clothes or in the traditional but simple bright cotton or silk costumes associated in the past with strolling companies of ballad-players and acrobats. Girls are in often pastel-shaded plain or patterned tops and plain coloured trousers, boys in more ordinary but very clean working clothes — boiler suit, peasant shirt and neck-towel, army uniform, student casuals and spectacles, whichever suits the part. Red on the face and heavy black on the eyebrows, which is supposed to give their features boldness, is all the make-up they normally wear.

A two-and-a-half hour programme by amateur propaganda teams from various departments of Peking University on 1 June 1973 (the fifty-second anniversary of the founding of the Communist Party) consisted of fourteen items written and performed by worker-peasant-soldier students and teachers. Among them, a dance, *Peoples of All China's Nationalities Praise Chairman Mao*, urged national unity. A song with dance and tableaux (*piao yen chang*), *Celebrate Chairman Mao's Instruction 'Keep fit and study well'*, referred to Mao's message to the students of the first enrolment after the universities reopened in 1970 following the cultural revolution. A chorus, *Workers of Taching Are Full of Energy*, appealed to everyone to copy the Taching oilmen's self-reliance and perseverance when facing difficult conditions. A song with marching and tableaux, *We Are Future Geologists*, stressed that scientific research is a form of serving the people. A comic clapper-talk (*kuai pan*), *Visiting the Family*, showed a student going home in the vacation and proudly telling his naively misunderstanding relatives what study at a university was really like. A song with tableaux, *Worker-peasant-soldier Students Are Loyal to the Party for Ever* reasserted the need for Party discipline over the students, many of whom had been rebellious Red Guards. A clapper-talk, *Soviet Revisionists Are Ugly-faced*, made fun of Russian 'social-imperialism'. A song with rhyme and gestures (*tan hsien*), *Never Forget Class Struggle*, repeated Mao's theory of continuing the revolution under socialism. A chorus praised Albanian comrades-in-arms. A tenor solo, *I Love the Blue Sea*, exulted in the sailor's life — many students of the 1970 intake came from the armed services. A piece for flute with an accompaniment of traditional instruments was called *Busy Sending Grain to the State on a Horse-drawn Cart*.

Above: *Agitational sketches: actresses and orchestra of the Peking Opera Company of Liaoning province staging an item criticizing Confucius and Lin Piao in a street in Shenyang city in 1974.* (pp. 21, 116)

Below: *Children's drama: a Little Red Soldiers propaganda team in Nanking entertains workers with a song and dance performance underlining the worker-peasant alliance.* (p. 32)

Many cultural troupes run by the army, navy and air force of the P.L.A. are full-time and the singers and musicians for them come from the professional variety stage, as well as from the drama schools and music academies.

In periods of maximum political and social upheaval — the wars, the Great Leap Forward, the cultural revolution — the agitational sketch achieves a much more independent and assertive existence as a medium of propaganda and agitation which can have a direct influence on quickly-changing day-to-day events. At such times an agitational item is written in a matter of minutes, rehearsed at once and performed the same day; and perhaps the next day it will be scrapped in favour of a new piece. In periods of less urgent political activity, when their function is to spread more generalized propaganda, agitational sketches consolidate and deepen; techniques improve, scripts are circulated, items are polished and reperformed and models even begin to appear. The most successful items are chosen for performance at May Day and National Day (1 October) festivities in the parks of towns and cities. Some are adopted by the professional stage and incorporated into variety shows.

Variety Shows

Amateur and professional song and dance troupes, cultural troupes and propaganda teams attached to factories and communes and more especially to the higher level administrative units — counties, provinces, municipalities and bureaux in the capital — give regular variety shows in city theatres, Workers' Palaces, trade union halls, and communes. All the elements of Chinese popular theatre may be combined in these two-and-a-half to three-hour shows. The usual items are short song and dance dramas in Chinese national minority and western ballet styles; comic cross-talk (*hsiang sheng*), clapper-talk (*kuai pan*) and other forms of ballad and story-telling known as *chuyi*; musical solos and orchestral works on western and traditional Chinese instruments; solo songs and choruses in national and western styles; massed choirs in Russian style; agitational and political sketches, slogans and tableaux; and group recitations of political poetry.

Troupes under various bureaux and ministries are normally full-time, and, like the P.L.A. troupes, employ professional artists. The items in these and the P.L.A. performances are often confined to instrumental music and revolutionary songs for tenor and soprano, whereas variety shows in theatres around the time of the national festival days may have a very wide programme indeed, adding acts by jugglers, conjurers, magicians, animal-imitators, ventriloquists, strongmen, lion-dancers and acrobats to the usual items.

In the 1950s and early 1960s the Shanghai Great World Amusement Palace and similar entertainment centres in other cities showed a variety of performances under one roof. On small stages simultaneous productions of operas, modern dramas (especially one-act plays), acrobatics and variety would go on every evening and weekend. These centres were closed in 1966. The Shanghai Great World reopened in 1973 as a Youth Palace run by the city's Communist Youth League. Besides lectures, exhibitions and sports, the Palace puts on *chuyi*, acrobatics and performances by local amateur propaganda teams. Young people also perform their own plays. Workers' palaces in city districts do similar work.

Acrobatics

For centuries despised by scholars, who regarded popular drama as a low art and acrobatics as the lowest of all, this very ancient form acquired new status as popular entertainment after 1949. Once struggling to survive, companies are now supported by city and provincial authorities and they are to be found even in some county towns and villages. Regional styles have been somewhat standardized and the shows of the best professional companies, though technically outstanding, are over-produced, especially those that have been carefully prepared for touring abroad: costumes and decor are prettified, movement is streamlined at the expense of meaning and the winsome, charming smiles of the acrobats are indiscriminate and unrelenting. It is often better to see these companies, or their number two teams of trainees and less-skilled players, performing in the hot sun before an audience of peasants resting from their work on the threshing ground. There is then no attempt at archness and the fresh grace and technical brilliance of the players can be seen without gloss as being born of superb physical discipline and an unassuming but total commitment to perfection.

After a brief period of reorientation during the cultural revolution, when many troupes were disbanded and the remainder injected political content into their performances, professional acrobatic companies returned to the stage in 1970 with items condemned as feudal or superstitious three years before, such as magicians' acts and the lion dance, restored to their programmes. In compliance with a new line of foreign policy and taking advantage of an international climate more favourable to China, the government sent five major acrobatic companies to tour more than thirty western and third-world countries in 1972—74.

Circus acts with animals faced a similar period of disapproval and circuses as such remain disbanded. However, individual acts with horses, monkeys and bears were introduced into the programme of the Peking Acrobatic Company at May Day performances in 1973.

Acrobatic troupes on tour within China perform wherever a mobile stage can conveniently be set up in the villages. In cities and towns they use theatres, stadia, and the auditoria available in most work-places. A performance, lasting two hours, normally contains twelve to fifteen items.

A performance by the Peking Acrobatic Company at the Capital Theatre on 21 March 1973 contained seventeen items: a prologue, featuring banners, streamers and lanterns; men's gymnastics (twelve men); diabolo (five women); balancing on a tower of bricks (two women); conjuring (one woman); magic, and comic talk, in front of the curtain during a scene change (two men); tight-rope walking (two women); leaping through hoops (five men); trick cycling (eleven-year-old girl, ten-year-old boy, with ten men and women); more comic magic; traditional magic (one man, two women); plate spinning (twelve women); spinning water-filled bowls (one man, one woman); balancing on a tower of chairs (one woman); balancing bowls (two men); balancing bowls on the head while doing gymnastics (one woman); lion dance (six men). An orchestra of Chinese traditional instruments accompanied each act.

Puppet and Shadow Theatre

String, rod and glove puppet companies perform in various regional styles. Fukien string puppets are well-known for the complexity of their movements. Canton rod puppets are about one metre high with carved wooden heads. Szechuan's are life-size.

Above: *May Day in the parks: minority dances and workers' dances in the park of the Working People's Palace of Culture, part of the old Imperial Palace, Peking.* (p. 23)

Below: Puppet Orchestra, *an item by the Peking Puppet Company, using rod puppets.* (p. 25)

Today the Peking Puppet Company's rod puppets are best known. They are about one metre high. Three rods attached to the head and wrists support the body and control the arms. The heads are made from papier-mache by skilled handicraftsmen. Most of the puppets are footless but the legs, hands, fingers, head, mouth and eyes can be made to move. These features are best shown in the item *Puppet Orchestra*, which has a dozen puppets playing traditional and western instruments while a backstage orchestra provides the sound.

Modern stories have replaced the feudal tales and legends. The programme of the Peking Puppet Company at the Changan Theatre on 1 January 1973, given by eight women and four men puppeteers and twenty musicians, had six items: a table-tennis match between two boys; a play in eight scenes, *The Cock Crows at Midnight*, adapted from the autobiographical story by Kao Yu-pao about poor peasants' vengeance against a cruel landlord, whose bald head swells visibly after a severe beating; a dance by seven Little Red Soldier girls to the popular children's song *Everyone Loves Peking's Tien An Men*; a Korean minority song and dance, *The People of Yinpien Love Chairman Mao*; a Tibetan song and dance, *A Golden Sun Shines in Peking*; and a play in three scenes, *Little Guerrillas*, about children liberation fighters in South Vietnam. The coloured back projections of landscapes, together with the rectangular frame of the proscenium arch, five metres wide and two metres high — raised so that the spectators in the front seats had to gaze up — created the appearance of a wide-screen colour film. This impression was reinforced by the shadowless, glaring lighting. Although the stories were obviously intended for children, the audience consisted mainly of adults. The company also goes out to tour schools.

Another successful puppet play by the same troupe, *Red Flowers on the Grasslands*, which was played on 1 June (Children's Day) 1973 in Peking's Children's Palace, was about children saving sheep and exposing dangerous 'bad elements' on the Mongolian steppe, a theme that started life as an opera, written by the Peking Opera Company of the Inner Mongolian Art Theatre, and recurs in a film cartoon, picture story-books and a ballet. The three scenes featured a number of animals — an eagle, horses and carts and a camel, besides lambs and sheep. Lantern-slides of storms, huts and grassland landscapes were projected on the back cloth. The puppeteers spoke the lines and sang the songs. The words of the songs were projected on to a screen at the side of the stage.

Shadow puppets are flat, a third of a metre high figures cut from donkey skin that has been tanned until it is translucent and then coloured. The coloured shadow of these figures is thrown on to a screen, formerly paper or cloth but now of opaque glass. The heads, usually depicted in profile, are detachable to allow for costume changes. The arms, legs and hands are articulated. The puppet is held flat against the screen by a central wire attached to the neck and by two other wires joined to each hand. With these three wires the puppet is manipulated. Words, songs and music are supplied by the puppeteers and a small group of musicians sitting behind the screen. Regional shadow styles differ in dialect, music and movements.

The old shadow plays used the characters of the feudal operas with their colourful robes, masks and painted faces. These and certain characters special to the shadow theatre — ushers of souls, ferocious temple guardians, assorted spectres from the underworld of Chinese mythology, as well as the dragon, the fox demon and other legendary animals — were well-suited to the shadow screen. Mobile troupes entertained rich families in their homes on festive occasions and provided fantasies for the entertainment of secluded court ladies.

With its origin in ancient times thought to have been in the spiritualistic summoning of the shades of the ancestors, shadow theatre presented a strange, ethereal world — probably the most difficult of all the traditional forms to adapt to modern, revolutionary use. A few old stories, such as *The Pilgrimage to the West* — celebrating the exploits of the mythical Monkey King, Sun Wu-kung, and his attacks on the White-bone Demon, who appeared in various sympathetic disguises such as a beautiful girl or an old woman — retained some symbolic usefulness after 1949.

Before liberation, puppet troupes struggled to exist in a countryside crippled by economic chaos. All but one of the shadow troupes were extinct by 1948. The new government moved quickly to restore and sponsor both puppet and shadow companies in the capital and the provinces. A National Puppet Theatre was founded in 1953. By 1954 there were some 1,000 troupes in operation. In 1955 a festival of puppet and shadow drama presented fifty-five plays on historical subjects with contemporary meanings. New plays with contemporary stories emerged in the next five years. Typical was the shadow play *Battling the Waves on the Lotus River at Night* (1958) which contained propaganda both for equal status for women and for the backyard steel campaign of the Great Leap Forward: charcoal is delivered by boat to the furnaces by four girls who manoeuvre their craft through some dangerous rapids which previously the locals said only men could negotiate. The new shadow plays were perhaps not found artistically or politically successful and shadow theatre was slow to revive on a national scale after the cultural revolution. However, a number of provincial troupes were represented at the National Puppet Theatre Festival in 1975 with plays adapted from the model Peking operas.

While both puppet and shadow plays resemble the operas of the living stage and troupes have always borrowed freely from Peking and local opera stories, it is known that both forms long pre-dated opera, which cannot therefore be their origin. Rather the reverse: very likely, as Mei Lan-fang believed, the highly stylized puppet-like gestures and movements of the opera stage find their origin in these ancient arts.

Story-telling and Balladry (chuyi)

Perhaps the most ancient of all popular narrative arts is the telling of stories in prose or rhymed ballads (*chuyi*, literally 'tuneful art'). In China, as in other countries with predominantly peasant populations, this art has persisted to the present day with remarkable vigour despite the disdain of the scholars. The power of the story-teller was recognized from the outset of the communist revolution when the Red Army propaganda troupes in the Kiangsi base used the form to spread the anti-feudal struggle. Later, sung and chanted stories and ballads were collected and studied in Yenan by folk-art specialists of the Lu Hsun Academy. The writer, Ting Ling, described the Shensi story-tellers of those days: 'The stories are sung to music by blind musicians. They have a *pipa*, a kind of guitar with four strings. There is a kind of flat board laced to the leg beneath the knees — they can tap on it with their fingers to give an accompaniment, or else they can beat on it with a bronze clapper, or else they have a sounding board above the knee to beat on. They sing without gestures, an interminable story of heroes of the past, of kings and the downfall of dynasties, of amazing battles and great deaths.'[9] Stories of peasant resistance to the Japanese soon entered their repertoire.

Today items appear in variety shows and agitational performances. Whole programmes given by professional *chuyi* artists draw big audiences in Shanghai and Peking theatres. Radio and television has enabled local styles to be heard throughout the country. Worker and peasant amateur propaganda teams experiment with new content which combines humour with revolutionary positiveness. Satire is avoided except by those who 'dare to go against the tide.' Rural amateurs no longer stroll from village to village; they perform for their commune. Mobile professional teams which include story-tellers are strongly centralized and move by lorry, bus and train from the cities and towns through the villages.

It is claimed there are over 200 local varieties of *chuyi*. The *ping hua* story form, unaccompanied by music, is performed, often by a woman, with the aid of gestures, facial expressions and occasionally a song. The *tan tzu* is a narration with an accompaniment on a *san hsien*, a three-stringed, long-necked instrument played either by the narrator or a supporting musician; sometimes a *pipa* is added. The *ta ku shu* is performed to the beat of a small drum and a pair of wooden clappers. *Kuai pan*, popular in the north, is a rhymed story recited to the beat of bamboo clappers. *Kuai shu* is a rhythmical narration in Shantung dialect, with metal clappers. The *hsiang sheng* is a comic, sometimes satirical monologue or dialogue in rapid vernacular in which there are two characters, one wise, who carries the narrative, and one foolish, who is his foil. When the piece is a monologue, the single actor plays both characters and this can add to the humour, as well as the skill, of the cross-talk.

While solo and duo performances are common, certain forms of ballad suitable for groups are increasingly popular. The *tan hsien*, once a ballad sung to the accompaniment of a one-stringed fiddle, is now virtually a ballad opera: a group, often amateurs and usually women, perform in alternating speech and song punctuated by balletic freezes and traditional mime and gesture. The performance achieves a smooth-flowing pattern of movement governed by the speech rhythms and accompanied in the sung passages by an orchestra of traditional Chinese instruments, plus a viola, situated offstage. Similar is *piao yen chang*, a group song with gestures and stylized movements.

In these dramatic stories the heroes are workers intent on raising production or, as in the *tan hsien*, *Story of Wang*, by the Amateur Propaganda Team of Tahsing County, peasants who aim to overcome their poverty by collective self-reliance, bitter political struggle and sheer hard work.

Professionals have been experimenting with ballads for instrumental groups. In Shanghai eleven girls from the Philharmonic Society, all graduates of the city's Conservatoire of Music, sit on stage in pleated skirts, white blouses and high-heeled sandals, playing the *pipa*, the *juan* (a two-stringed banjo), the *cheng* (a many-stringed zither), the *yang chin* (dulcimer) and the *erh hu* (two-stringed fiddle), and sing a ballad, now in unison, now in turns, interrupted by musical interludes or by short bursts of dialogue in soft southern dialects. Their subjects are militiawomen doing drill and the political and production struggles of women weavers.

Children's Drama

Children's dramatic societies were organized and trained by teenage Young Vanguards in the north Shensi villages after the Long March of 1935. They propagandized the United Front of the communists with the Kuomintang and praised the exploits of the Eighth Route Army. A troupe of twenty-four Shanghai children aged nine to nineteen, calling themselves the Children's Dramatic Club, toured central China by boat and on foot during the anti-Japanese war showing short plays with such titles as *Final Victory*, *Arrest the Traitors*, *Aid Our Mobile Units*, *Solidarity* and *On the Firing Line*. In the communist areas during the War of Liberation young people were encouraged to write and act their own plays to aid the war and the land reform.

After liberation the communists always included drama among the activities for Young Pioneers and the Youth League, but at the same time there grew up a more fanciful and sentimental tradition, deriving from Hollywood as much as from the Russian children's theatre. Plays for children, rather than by them, dominated. Legends and fantasies, moral and pretty, were put on at the Peking Children's Theatre. *Magic Aster* (1963), a three-act drama by Jen Teh-yao, was an exciting fantasy with a pantomime of Disney animals — spotted doe, fawn, monkey, squirrel and mermaids. This coy tradition survives today in children's cartoon films, less in the subject matter than in the style of drawing and colouring.

In the cultural revolution most children deserted such plays and turned to agitational sketches which they wrote, produced and acted themselves, under the guidance of local radicals. By 1969 these children had been organized by Party and army representatives and drama teachers into Mao Tse-tung Thought Propaganda Troupes, the most famous of which were in Nanking, where there were twenty groups, two for each of the ten districts of the city. One group in each district was composed of primary school children (Little Red Soldier Troupes) and one of children from middle schools (Red Guard Troupes). The city today has in addition one special troupe, made up of the best children drawn from the different districts into a single school so they can rehearse and perform together.

In Shanghai the troupe attached to the Chingan Children's Palace attained great skills, especially in mime in a lorry-driving item, in a rice-transplanting song and dance, a militia drill *Song of the Red Spears*, and a dance by four girls in light blue-and-white spotted trousers, scarlet blouses and tiny yellow aprons, who embroidered on pink paper embroidery frames the words 'A Long Life to Chairman Mao'.

A programme by the Hsinhua District Little Red Soldiers Troupe of Shihchiachuang city, Hopei province, on 27 October 1972, had sixteen items: a song and dance, a *tan hsien* about a lost girl being found by a soldier, a red-scarf dance, a comic mime by Little Red Barbers washing and cutting their schoolmates' hair, a comic mime by a Carpenters' Group who make their own simple furniture, a song of washing clothes with a dance in Tibetan style, excerpts from the Peking opera *The Red Lantern* and the ballet *Red Detachment of Women*, a folk song *Ode to Liberation* and other solos and choruses.

Districts in most cities and large towns now have Little Red Soldier — or Littlé Red Guard — and Red Guard propaganda troupes which perform their sketches both at schools and before adults in communes, factories, mines and construction sites, and before soldiers. Kindergartens and even nurseries, which are attached to most factories and other work places, have teams of infants who put on similar items at festivals and for visitors. Many young children are again being trained in the ancient military art of *wushu*, mainly variations on sword dances. A variety of children's items can be seen in parks as part of the celebrations on May Day and National Day. On Children's Day they give performances in Children's Palaces.

Ballet

The Chinese set great store by their revolutionization of western ballet. Few are the foreigners who are not taken to *Red Detachment of Women* while they are in Peking. While this may partly arise from a desire to contrast their own revolutionary offerings with the sedate conservatism of the Bolshoi Ballet's *Swan Lake* — the parallel entertainment for official guests in Moscow — there is little doubt that the China Dance Drama Company and Chiang Ch'ing, its main adviser before her overthrow, consider they are making a major contribution to the development of modern art.

The influence before 1949 was the English ballet through Tai Ai-lien who studied at Dartington Hall. Tai set up the Chinese Ballet Group in Chungking during the anti-Japanese war and after liberation she became head of the Peking School of Dance where Russian choreographers worked as advisers. Though the influence of classical ballet was strong and Chinese productions of *Le Corsaire*, *Swan Lake* and *Giselle* were given, attempts were made to incorporate traditional Chinese dance forms in a ballet *The Maid from the Sea*. But the ballet companies still tended to be bourgeois enclaves. Ballet dancers found their art little appreciated when they toured the countryside. What the Chinese cultural leaders felt was needed before the foreign form could meet the approval of the millions of workers and peasants was a radically altered content — a Chinese story and a revolutionary theme.

The first performance of *Red Detachment of Women*, a tale of the guerrilla struggle of women on the southern island of Hainan, was given on National Day, 1 October 1964, and it was followed during and after the cultural revolution by *The White-haired Girl*, *Ode to Yimeng* and *Children of the Grassland*, all on rural themes. While western ballet steps and instruments still predominate, the contribution of Chinese national and minority dance steps and instruments is stronger. The shows tell much more of a story than is common in western ballet and perhaps for that reason, in translation, the Chinese often use 'dance drama' as a preferable term to 'ballet'. Indeed, with the introduction of songs at certain points to underline the message of the dance, and the stress on colourful and energetic group dances based on folk styles, the ballets even resemble musicals.

Musicals (*Song and Dance Dramas*)

Owing something to the *yangko* musical dramas which were developed in Yenan, such as *Brothers and Sisters Open up Wasteland*, *The White-haired Girl* and *Red Leaves River*, full-length song and dance dramas are performed by professional and amateur ensembles in city theatres, using stories with tensely dramatic, fast and simple plotlines. With their spectacular realistic scenery, technicolour lighting and maximum melodrama, they also owe something to American musicals. They have incorporated some of the spectacle of traditional Chinese opera, especially the fighting and tumbling. Often on international themes, they were widespread during the cultural revolution but appear to have declined since. *War Drums on the Equator* (Congo), *Letters from the South* (Vietnam), *Flames of Anger over the Coconut Groves* (Vietnam) and *Storm over the Andes* offered some opportunity for the ensembles to experiment with make-up, character portrayal and folk music of other countries. Some of these musicals also appeared as modern dramas. Built round short melodramatic scenes often featuring a U.S. imperialist with red hair and long nose, tall, drunk and easily outwitted, they rise to a climax with a spectacular fight involving the imperialist and local liberation fighters played by skilled acrobats. All end with a tableau and shouted slogans affirming the universal victory of people's war, against a cyclorama of billowing smoke and angry flames. The internal politics of the cultural revolution were dealt with in *The January Storm* (from Shanghai), *Dawn in the North-east* (from Harbin) and *Spring Thunder in the South-west* (from Kweiyang). The earlier and even more spectacular *The East Is Red* (1964), with a cast of 1,000 actors and 1,000 singers, told the epic history of the Chinese Communist movement.

With any future renewal of the people's war theme in Party policy, it is likely that full-length song and dance dramas will return. Meanwhile, some song and dance ensembles have gone over to performing shorter items with little plot and more influence from western ballet. They are more in the nature of celebratory and exhortative pieces.

They praise peasants for a good harvest and workers for increased production, encourage the militia, propagate social reform in Tibet, and, as in *Like Fish and Water* (1972) — literally, 'Fish/Water Feeling' — by the Cultural Troupe of the Political Department of the P.L.A. Railway Corps, urge a greater identity of feelings between soldiers and the people.

The songs and dances of China's fifty-five national minorities remain a regular feature of programmes both in city theatres and on rural tours. In these items, actors of the majority Han race dress up in the splendid national costumes of the minorities and perform to the popular tunes of Inner Mongolia, Tibet and Sinkiang, the Yis and Thais from the south-west, the Koreans from the north-east and other areas. Uighur music, perhaps the furthest removed from Han styles, is among the most played.

The Song and Dance Troupe of the Central Institute of National Minorities provides the Peking stage with performances by folk artists who are teaching or training at the Institute. A dance by the Institute's arts department that was popular in 1973, *Taking Grain to the State*, shows the solidarity of Thai and Chingpo peoples who help each other grow rice. Song and dance ensembles of the remoter provinces travel the country with similar items. In December 1964 a month-long festival of amateur songs and dances of the minorities was held in Peking and recorded on film.

The Han culture is rather short of popular dances. The tuneful and colourful folk styles of the minorities compensate for that lack and infuse new ideas into the Han traditions. At the same time, the cultivation of the minority styles has the political purpose of encouraging pride in the vastness and richness of China and its culture, and of strengthening national unity.

Companies

The great majority of companies are local, regional and provincial groups of amateurs and professionals who will certainly tour but who will not move out of their given areas except to attend drama festivals. They are attached to the cultural bureaux of the administration at the levels of province, autonomous region or municipality, county and commune, and are financed by them. Those lower than the commune level are attached to the production brigade, the equivalent

Above: *The unity of the people: song and dance drama,* Like Fish and Water, *by the Cultural Troupe of the People's Liberation Army Railway Corps. Soldiers on manoeuvres and village women do good deeds for each other.* (pp. 35, 106)

Below: *Adapting Peking operas to local forms: a* huaichu *version of* On the Docks *performed by the Shanghai Huaichu Company for dock workers of No. 5 Wharf, Shanghai.* (pp. 48, 84–5, 96–7)

of the old village or group of villages. Those lower than the municipal or other city administration are attached to the district administration or even to the neighbourhood or street. Factory, office and school companies are under the various industrial, commercial and educational bureaux. At all levels they are supervised by the members of the revolutionary and Party committees responsible for cultural affairs. A number of companies are attached to units of the P.L.A.

Some of the larger professional companies of the big municipalities of Peking and Shanghai, while still being administered by their respective municipal revolutionary committees, have been singled out for a special relationship with the Cultural Group under the State Council — the old Ministry of Culture, dissolved in the cultural revolution and restored in 1975 — and count more or less as national companies. They receive considerable amounts of state aid, both financially and politically. It is through them that cultural policies are put to the test, thus giving to the top drama companies of China more political function, and hence more influence over the way the culture shall or shall not go, than is perhaps to be found in any other country. Of these the China Peking Opera Company, the Peking Opera Companies of Peking and Shanghai and the China Dance Drama Company are the most important. They have pioneered the experiments in revolutionizing the Peking opera and the ballet, from which have since flowed most of the major changes in the other fields of dramatic art.

Local operas are, of course, represented by local companies. For *huachu*, the major cities each support a professional company; those of Peking and Tientsin have been prominent recently. The national China Modern Drama Company emerged in 1974. A Peking Variety Company was in existence in 1971 but its functions seem now to have been divided among the city's acrobatic, puppet, song and dance and *chuyi* troupes. Acrobatics were represented abroad during 1972–74 by companies from Peking, Wuhan, Shenyang, Kwangchow and Shanghai; but many other cities and counties have troupes, outstanding examples being those from Changchou and Tientsin. The Peking Puppet Company is now the model for the many others of its type in the provinces, as is the Peking Chuyi Company. The China Song and Dance Ensemble is a national company but neither shadow theatre nor children's drama appears to be represented nationally at the present time.

The leading opera and ballet companies of Peking, Shanghai and other cities, and students of drama and dance schools, spend about three months each year in factories and communes, showing opera and ballets, labouring at work-benches and in the fields and teaching local amateurs. The Pingchu and Peking Opera Companies of Peking, doing their rural stint of 1971, divided up into small groups and went to out-of-the-way valleys near the city not only to perform for the peasants but also to carry water, sweep yards, cut hair and repair farm equipment.

Mobile Theatre

In the more remote and sparsely populated areas of the west and north-west, mobile troupes are on constant tour. An eighteen-member professional Red Propaganda Team on the Pamir Plateau climbs ice-covered precipices 6,000 metres above sea-level to perform for Tajik herdsmen. In Tibet young amateurs — sons and daughters of emancipated serfs — and professionals of the Tibet Song and Dance Ensemble tour the communes denouncing serfdom and pointing out to peasants the advantages of growing winter wheat. In the mountains of Kweichow, members of the Bamboo Basket Theatrical Troupe carry their props in baskets on their backs.

Perhaps the most famous of all the mobile troupes, the Ulan Muchir of Inner Mongolia, tours the banners (pastoral areas) and counties (agricultural areas) of the grasslands and deserts all the year round, carrying its simple props and musical instruments on horse-back and camel-back to the nomads' tents, scattered settlements and border guard-posts. Larger regional troupes travel by horse-cart. The professional Inner Mongolian Regional Ulan Muchir travelled 3,500 kilometres in three months in summer 1973, performing for over 200,000 people. While halted, the players worked alongside the herdsmen, dug wells, built sheep pens, milked the goats and cows, herded the horses and cut hay.

Joining in labour while on tour is a traditional feature of China's revolutionary drama groups. Art troupes in the Kiangsi base in the early 1930s helped peasants with spring sowing. Mobile troupes in Yenan in the 1940s opened up wasteland, cultivated the virgin soil and harvested the grain. In the late 1950s, the eighty-four-strong Shehsien Hsiao Laotzu Company of southern Hopei took its local operas to tiny hamlets in the Taihang Mountains where they found old women, confined to the hill-tops by their bound feet, who had never before seen a play. This troupe spent four days in each place: they performed every evening, rehearsed for two days, and laboured in the fields or helped build reservoirs for the other two. They also found time to coach village amateurs[10]. This is probably the pattern of work for most of the thousands of touring troupes in China's countryside.

Mobile theatre is not confined to the remoter parts. In the rich and heavily populated ricelands of Kiangsi province, it was said in 1973 that there were more than 5,000 peasant artists in one county alone, playing in village clubs, at reservoir sites, threshing grounds and everywhere they could muster an audience[11]. They had a total repertoire of 2,200 songs, dances, pieces of music, short plays, ballads and operas which they had composed themselves since 1968. Often making their own fiddles and drums, they pitched their stories close to the life and struggle of the people: the bitterness of the past, the next harvest, and the political movements against feudal and bourgeois ideas were recurring themes. Some of these artists show noteworthy powers of innovation. Once, while a troupe from Hsiayang production brigade was performing, they heard the radio forecast a rain storm. They interrupted their show to help the peasants to cover the grain drying on the threshing ground, and, returning to the stage, inserted an impromptu ballad into the programme, *Racing against Rain*. Another player has shown ingenuity of a different sort: a nineteen-year-old peasant of the Ssupu brigade plays songs and local opera arias on ten porcelain bowls with a pair of chopsticks.

Theatre Buildings

Most Chinese see plays either in the open air in the fields, the village street or the commune yard, or in the auditorium of their factory. Cultural Parks and Cultural Palaces in a number of cities provide stages mainly for amateurs. In the county towns, provincial cities and municipalities, however, there are theatres, the majority built since 1949. In these theatres the proscenium arch is universal. The buildings are functional, with adequate lighting systems, a wide but often shallow stage and a one- or two-storeyed auditorium.

Although in terms of quantity and perhaps also of variety there is a great deal of activity in the provinces, where indeed grassroots theatre is to be found, the Chinese regard Peking as unquestionably the leading city of the Chinese theatre, a showcase of model productions and the political and organizational centre of drama development. Shanghai has played a unique leading role at various times, especially just before and during the cultural revolution, but in general it comes second to Peking.

Of Peking's theatres the oldest building still in use is the small Changan Theatre on Changan Boulevard, the wide main street that crosses Peking from east to west. Built about sixty years ago for performances of traditional opera, the intimacy of this single-storey auditorium, seating about 300, is suited to the puppet shows, *chuyi* ballads and concerts that are currently played there.

The largest and one of the newest theatres is the main auditorium of the Great Hall of the People, built in 1958, which seats 6,000. The spectacle *The East Is Red* was staged there but nowadays it is only used by foreign companies invited by the government from countries whose Communist Party has special political relations with the Chinese Communist Party. In 1972—74 dance and opera troupes from Korea, Albania and Romania played there.

Of the other venues for large-scale performances, the Workers' Stadium in the northern suburbs is used for mass callisthenics displays. The Workers' Gymnasium has shown acrobatics and circus acts on festival days. The Capital Stadium has given exhibition performances of *wushu* and it is also the site of the variety performances that open and terminate China's international table-tennis tournaments. In Peking's parks, especially the gardens of the Imperial Palace, the Summer Palace, the Temple of Heaven and Tao Jan Ting, hundreds of amateur and professional troupes gather on May Day and National Day to show several thousand short items on temporary stages.

Of the conventional Peking theatres, the Theatre of the Industrial Exhibition Hall, seating about 2,000, is the largest. It shows programmes of music, songs, dances, *chuyi* and other short items which, after the festivals, are chosen from among the best shown in the parks. A similar function is performed by the Theatre of the Palace of the National Minorities, which seats 1,600.

Among the big companies, the China Peking Opera Company plays at the Capital Theatre, the People's Theatre and the February Seventh Theatre. The Capital has also housed the Peking Acrobatic Company and received a number of visiting folk song and dance companies from Third World countries. Performances of *chetzuhsi* and *pingchu* opera have been given there. The Workers' Club Theatre is the home of the Peking Opera Company of Peking. The China Dance Drama Company puts on its ballets at the Tienchiao Theatre in south Peking's old entertainment district.

Local companies are represented by the Peking Modern Drama Company which plays *huachu* at the small East Is Red Theatre at the eastern end of Changan Boulevard, previously the Youth Art Theatre. This theatre also shows local Hopei *pangtzu* and Peking operas and it is very much a theatre for the local people. So is the East Wind Theatre in the narrow Goldfish Lane off Wangfuching, the central shopping street, which has shown the local-dialect comic *pingchu*, *Hsiangyang Store*, by the Peking Pingchu Company, and the Hopei *pangtzu* version of *Song of the Dragon River*. Another local group, the Peking Wind and Thunder Company, shows Peking operas at the Masses Theatre.

Other Peking theatres occupied during drama festivals include the Children's Theatre, the Rehearsal Theatre of the Central Dramatic Institute, the Physical Labour Theatre, the Red Flag Theatre and the auditoria of various government bureaux, army units, trade unions and district workers' clubs.

Most theatres are by no means used every evening. Indeed, because companies spend much of their time in the suburbs and the countryside, many theatres are closed for part of the summer and in the winter performances are sporadic. The main Peking theatres are open perhaps three nights a week from October to May except for the peak season for theatre-going, the Spring Festival at the end of January or beginning of February, when they will be open daily for several weeks and will sometimes play matinees as well as evenings.

Seats in Peking theatres are block booked and tickets are distributed through the municipal cultural bureau on a rota basis to organizations in the city. With the exception of a permanent quota to the Foreign Ministry and other government departments for diplomats and visiting foreign delegations, the tickets are supplied first to factories through the trade unions and then to other organizations, offices, schools and universities. Only rarely are any tickets kept back for sale at the box office. Prices are low, perhaps fifty cents (about ten pence) for a seat in the middle stalls. A row of seats in the front stalls may be reserved for distinguished visitors and Chinese leaders but there is little price difference and there are no boxes. Tickets for May Day and National Day performances in the parks are allocated in a similar way.

Theatre Audiences

In the larger professional theatres of Peking probably a majority of theatre-goers are from the administration and intelligentsia. This is partly because a large proportion of the city's population is employed in state bureaux situated in the capital and there are relatively few industrial workers compared with, say, Shanghai. But it is also attributable to the fact that those who apply for tickets from their organizations are likely to be habitual theatre-goers and they will be mainly from the old bourgeoisie. This is most true of Peking opera audiences.

However, with the system of distributing tickets to organizations on a rota basis, the proportion of tickets going to organizations employing a high percentage of intellectuals is lower than would be the case if distribution were on a first-come, first-served sales basis. In addition experiments have been made within the organizations receiving tickets, either to allot tickets to employees on a rota basis, or to hold an election among employees to decide whose work or attitude merits the reward of a ticket, or, lastly, to award tickets to selected employees on similar grounds but without an election. As a result of these measures there has been a rise in the number of industrial and office workers visiting the professional theatre at least once a year, and a large minority of any audience at these theatres, and outside Peking often a majority, would be workers or worker-cadres and their families.

As for amateur performances — they are the great majority of performances — the entire audience would be of workers, peasants and worker- or peasant-cadres, with sometimes a handful of higher-level leaders and administrators. Such performances are free.

At drama festivals in the capital nearly two-thirds of the audiences are said to be workers, peasants and soldiers, the remainder being drama workers invited to share their experience with other drama workers.

Drama Training and Theatre Research

Most training is done by a veteran amateur in the village, teaching his skill to a trainee. At higher levels, the professional county troupes train their new recruits on the job, though trainees will obviously already have acquired some skills from local amateur artists. In addition professionals help to train amateurs while on tour with their companies.

In the cities, municipalities and the capital, the state-aided professional companies recruit most of their players from drama schools and music academies. The best known of the drama schools is the National School of Peking Opera, set up in 1952, which takes children at the age of ten or eleven and gives them a ten-year course. In the past a child was selected for a particular role and trained intensively for it. This was because the technique of the traditional opera was so complex. There were, for instance, fifty movements of the sleeve of a gown and twenty ways of laughing and smiling, all symbolic. But this tradition is weakening now that Peking opera has been revolutionized. Players are today encouraged to learn a wider range of parts. The school also trains musicians for the opera and in the 1950s it took in a further group of pupils at the age of sixteen and trained them for four years in the techniques of local opera. It is not clear whether it still does so or whether this duty has been delegated to other schools in Peking. The teachers are veteran opera actors and musicians, but the political guidance derives from the tradition of the Gorky School in Juichin and the Lu Hsun Academy in Yenan and finds its way to the pupils and the teachers through the school's Party committee.

In 1957 the National School of Peking Opera had 400 pupils. In 1959 the first graduates emerged, sixty-five in all. It was these graduates, and those of the succeeding four years, who came under the influence of 'the bourgeois line' while at school. Having been taught as many as sixty different traditional operas they had then to learn the new disciplines of the revolutionized operas during the cultural revolution.

Peking municipality had its own Peking opera school, established in 1952, though it may recently have been merged with the National School. Outside Peking there are schools of local opera in major cities, some of which teach Peking opera too. The Shanghai Municipal Opera School is one of these.

The main school of modern drama is Peking's Central Dramatic Institute, which opened in 1950 and teaches acting, stage production and design. Russian advisers who had been attached to the school in the early 1950s withdrew in 1960. The students, some of whom have had experience in amateur theatre before enrolling, are taught a form of the Stanislavsky Method, heavily modified since the cultural revolution, and after graduation they are posted to the professional modern drama companies in the capital and the provinces.

The Peking School of Dance, founded in 1954, trains dancers in classical ballet and in Chinese national and minority styles. Initially it operated with the help of Russian advisers. Pupils are taken between the ages of eleven and fourteen for a seven-year course. By 1962 there were some 200 instructors and over 300 students. After graduation students join the various professional dance drama and song and dance companies. A similar school of dance was opened in Shanghai in 1960. The arts department of the Central Institute of National Minorities in Peking offers students from the minority areas a three-year course in minority songs and dances, Han music and dances, and foreign ballet.

In 1974 the Peking School of Dance was incorporated under the Central May Seventh College of Arts, an organization which is also now responsible for the schools of opera and modern drama in Peking.

The China Institute of Dramatic Research was responsible for collecting and revising the scripts of traditional operas after 1950. Today its members concentrate more on research in the field of songs and dances of the minorities. They also advise on the adapting of the model Peking operas into local forms.

CHAPTER THREE

Characteristics of Contemporary Chinese Theatre

Contemporary Chinese drama is essentially a performing art and a collective one. Though texts are published they are not studied as the literary creation of one author or analysed in terms of language and expression. Based on one or more already created productions, texts are collective compositions printed as manuals for future productions. This is most true of the model works. As texts the models do not stand up well to reading. Little of their effect on stage can be guessed from the script alone. But the published 'model books' of the recent revolutionized Peking operas and ballets contain a full production scenario, providing text, music, photos of selected scenes, colour pictures of sets, close-ups of each character's facial type and make-up, illustrated lists of costumes and props and how to make them, a full plot of stage movements and business, and directions on stage effects and their coordination with the music.

The evolution of each model book is complex. The companies that are closest to the Cultural Group under the State Council — now once again the Ministry of Culture — work for several years on a production, giving trial performances before audiences from different social classes, until after much revision the production passes from its 'tentative' or 'experimental' stage and emerges as 'mature'. Once the text has been accepted by the Group as a model, the model book, incorporating the revisions, is published and handed down by the Group to the regional and local companies. Not only the text, therefore, but the entire production, as perfected by the leading companies, is regarded as a model for all other productions. The reverse process can also give rise to models: local opera companies work on local productions and then take them to the periodic drama festivals in the provincial capital or in Peking itself, for official approval and for possible adoption by the big companies for working up into models.

Such a model-oriented approach on the part of the cultural authorities indicates another and even more important characteristic of Chinese drama today: its didacticism. In the formulation of the Communist Party, cultural workers must use drama to help exercise the proletariat's dictatorship over the reactionary classes and to aid in the practice of democracy among the people. Productions are geared to whatever social and political struggle the Party deems necessary for a particular period. As conditions change and either the Party's or the people's thinking shifts, scripts are quickly outdated and need constant revision. Published scripts are nowadays given a date, recording when they were last revised. The July 1970 script of *Taking Tiger Mountain by Strategy*, for example, 'Revised collectively by the "Taking Tiger Mountain by Strategy" Group of the Peking Opera Company of Shanghai', is markedly different from the same company's version of 1967. The differences reflect the results of the political debate in the country as a whole in the intervening three years.

The role of Chinese drama as a function of political education is not at all simple. As in the past, drama has of course been monopolized since liberation by a few, both high and low in the cultural chain of command, and used as a tool to bolster their power. But in the last decade it has also proved its efficacy at doing the opposite — unseating them. The Confucian notion of the musical arts as something best played when things are going well for the rulers, so as to bind the people even more closely round them, is not yet dead in drama. But the really noteworthy characteristic of contemporary Chinese drama is its success in making conservatives uncomfortable. In short, its agitational function has often overridden its anaesthetizing tendency.

The function of drama as a motor of social change is a principle to which most theatre workers in China now subscribe and it is constantly repeated in official articles. 'China's artists try to generalize from complicated social phenomena (in order to evolve their themes) showing the essence of the struggle in life during a given historical period, so that their works can play the role of educating and encouraging the people,' said *Peking Review* summing up a festival of drama held in Peking in 1974.[12] 'The struggle in life' is of course class struggle which, since liberation in 1949, has taken on the form of 'the struggle between the socialist road and the capitalist road' — 'a protracted and complex' struggle, according to Mao, of which 'we must remind ourselves every year, every month and every day.'[13] Drama plays its part in this reminding.

Subscribing to such a principle is one thing; it is another to carry it out. When a veteran Peking opera actor of the traditional school finds his prestige and indeed the very foundations of his technique, which he has built up by constant labour ever since childhood, undermined, declared outdated by young critics, and his art branded as reactionary, it is difficult for him or her to feel enthusiasm for social change. After liberation some old-style actors retired and did not cooperate in reforming the old opera. Others concentrated on training young actors but gave up performing themselves. Some who continued finally ceased working during the cultural revolution, when the performance of traditional operas was stopped.

The younger generation of actors adapted somewhat better. The Szechuan opera actress, Chen Shu-fang, twenty-six at liberation, was trained from the age of seven to play feudal ladies. But she found that playing the part of the mother of a railway worker in *The Red Lantern* led her to a new identification with her audiences. The workers and peasants her company began to present on stage were the kind of people who made up the vast majority of her province's theatre-goers. She felt it was anomalous to parade herself in the robes of a court beauty in front of a brigade of 'iron girls' carrying buckets of earth to build a terraced field.[14]

In Mao's terms, for intellectuals, 'learning from the workers, peasants and soldiers precedes the task of educating them.' Ever since the Yenan days, and especially after liberation brought what the Communist Party claims is a socialist society, Mao has been anxious that 'We must not raise the workers, peasants and soldiers to the level of the feudal class, the bourgeoisie or the petty-bourgeois intelligentsia but along their own line of ascent, along the line of ascent of the proletariat.'[15]

There are problems in Mao's prescription. The peasants can hardly be expected to go along the line of ascent of the proletariat until they have been converted into proletarians. The workers might have expected that in a socialist society they could do their own 'raising' and not have intellectuals to do it for them. And among the intellectuals — the scholar class who follows the centuries-old custom of looking down on those who can, in Confucius' disparaging words, 'distinguish between the five grains' — elitism remains strong.

It is Party policy for intellectuals to 'remould themselves through physical labour'. The same actress, Chen Shu-fang, went to stay in the homes of peasants and worked in the fields. She became friendly with a formerly poor peasant woman and observed her pride in her job. 'It is useful for the collective,' explained the woman. A brick-kiln worker told her, 'It is labour that changes people.' Chen wrote, 'I was inspired to make my art into a weapon of the revolution.'

Another actress, Hung Hsien-nu, from a Kwangtung opera company, worked with Shanghai dockers while she was adapting the Peking opera *On the Docks* to the local Kwangtung style. 'My old way of singing didn't suit the people. Once I acted the role of a poor peasant woman giving advice to her child. I didn't know how she would think and feel and I used an aria from an old Peking opera, *A Concubine Teaches Her Son*. I confused the education in class struggle that a poor peasant would give her children with the maternal love of the feudal landlord class.' After working on the docks, 'My thinking and feelings began to change.' She was able successfully to play the scene in *On the Docks* where the woman Party secretary gives a lesson in class struggle to a young docker, one of the centrepieces of the opera.[16]

The young Peking opera actress, Li Ping-shu, revised her interpretation of the village Party secretary, Chiang Shui-ying, in *Song of the Dragon River*, after getting to know a peasants' daughter she met in Kelung village near Shanghai where her company spent several months in 1969—70. The girl, herself the village Party secretary, 'had no official air about her. She was warm and sincere. Peasants confided in her and told her their troubles. She never stopped working and she knew every family in the village. She was patient and always ready to help. I saw that the peasants' criticism of my interpretation of the role of Chiang Shui-ying was valid — "she puts on the airs of an intellectual". I resolved to change.' Li revised her interpretation and before long peasants seeing her in the fields would remark 'Here comes Party secretary Chiang Shui-ying.'

Li Ping-shu confessed, 'I once thought it easier to play in modern opera than the traditional. I need only walk and talk like my contemporaries. But I was wrong. At early rehearsals of *Song of the Dragon River*, I was at a complete loss what to do with my hands and feet. The feudal women I used to play were patterned on the conventions of the traditional theatre. But Chiang Shui-ying is a character familiar in life to the poor peasants and close to their hearts. If I was not in character on stage, the audience wouldn't accept the performance. What remains useful of the traditional opera techniques needs reforming. This is not merely a question of artistic creation but one of ideological revolution.'[17]

It is this ideological revolution, a change in thinking on the part of all workers in the field of drama, that is at the heart of the contemporary transformation of Chinese drama and gives to the new productions since the cultural revolution their freshness and, in the context of Chinese tradition, their startling and audacious novelty.

But mental remoulding, and the technical changes that follow it, is not confined to intellectuals from the bourgeoisie, neither is it something only professionals, and not amateurs, need to attend to. Workers are not 'born red'. They are open to petty bourgeois influence and also to the influence, through formal, ritualistic education at school and through their ancestral roots in the villages, of Confucian attitudes to authority. Most workers are still only one or two generations away from the soil and peasant obsequiousness may linger in them. 'If you employ upright officials, the people will be submissive. If one is sedate in their presence, they will be respectful. If you employ competent officials, the people will work hard,' said Confucius in the *Analects* and many Party officials have assumed Confucian robes. The vigorous upsurge of workers' amateur theatre in the past few years is the product of a difficult and prolonged mental revolutionization by the workers, who have had to give up revering not only cultural officials but also theatre professionals before they could launch out on their own path of dramatic expression.

The relationship between amateurs and professionals is sensitive and precarious. In years when the agitational function of drama is preponderant the professionals tend to retire to work on revolutionizing their art or merge into the turbulent crowd of workers' and peasants' amateur propaganda teams producing agitational plays. In years when there is a downward swing of the revolutionary pendulum the professionals emerge and develop their companies' work in accordance with the changed conditions.

To the advantage of the higher professionals is the security of their state-run companies which are required to stage regular productions good enough to show to visiting foreign dignitaries. The professionals lower down in the provinces and counties are likewise of some status and are expected to represent their area at local and national drama festivals. To the advantage of the amateurs is that their shows cost little, have strong local support in the factories and rural communes and, since they deal with local work problems, are closer to workers and peasants than the professionals' productions whose generalized themes tend to reflect national concerns.

Professionals and amateurs are officially supposed to learn from each others' good points on an equal footing but in reality the professionals are the 'power' whom the amateurs seek either to emulate or overthrow. The professionals regard the amateur companies as technically primitive while the officials fear them as cultural power bases that may escape their supervision. In the cultural revolution the worker and peasant amateurs, together with radical Party members and sympathizers among professional theatre workers, destroyed the old Ministry of Culture and briefly opened the way to a resurgence of agitational amateur theatre. The old chain of command has, however, re-emerged since, and the dominance of professionals has been reasserted. Amateur theatre today is officially assigned a more conservative function. There is scarcely a factory or commune without its spare-time art and propaganda troupe, emulating the professionals (in 1971 the Peking Opera Company of Peking, for example, assisted in the rehearsal of over 200 amateur propaganda teams) and bending to Party discipline whether the current Party line is 'correct' or not. They fulfil more of a cultural and less of an agitational role in society. In a few workplaces amateur plays are still vehicles for political criticism by drama workers who, in Mao's words, are brave enough to 'go against the tide' when the line is wrong.

While stopping short of workers' control, the cultural revolution has, however, forced on the reluctant professionals a greater participation by ordinary people and audiences in the making of plays. Material for professional productions is often still found in other plays or even other arts. *The Red Lantern* was first a modern drama, a film and a local Shanghai opera before finding fame as a Peking opera. *Taking Tiger Mountain by Strategy* was taken from a best-selling adventure story, *Tracks in the Snowy Forest* by Chu Po. *Shachiapang* started as a local opera in Shanghai called *Sparks amid the Reeds* before adaptation to Peking opera form. *Fighting on the Plains* started as a film. The one-act Shaohsing opera *Half a Basket of Peanuts* was adapted from a Chekiang *wuchu* opera which in turn derived from a short play, *Philosophy Blossoms in a Mountain Village*, written by workers in a meter and gauge factory in Hangchow. *Red Detachment of Women* evolved from a film through a ballet to a Peking opera. But once a tentative theme or plot is found it is worked up by writers who seek the advice and help of workers and peasants. In 1964 Mao's wife, Chiang Ch'ing, recommended the formation of 'a three-way combination of the leadership, the playwrights and the masses' for writing plays and this is still the prescription the companies follow.

Wang Shu-yüan, leader of the writing team attached to the Peking Opera Company of Peking, did research for *Azalea Mountain* in the mountainous region of south China in which this drama of the early days of the revolution is set. He listened to the stories of old peasants who had seen the birth of the Red Army there in 1928. Their tales had the common theme that 'making revolution relies on guns, and the guns must follow the Party.' On this basis Wang and his team built up their play. It warns of the dangers of the military controlling the Party and of 'the small bandit-group mentality' among the peasants. Its heroine is Ko Hsiang, the local Party representative, who had 'the daring and ability to oppose wrong trends.'[18] It is no coincidence that this opera appeared in its latest form in 1972 following the attempt by Marshal Lin Piao and the leaders of the armed forces to take over the administration from the Party. The play warned the people to recognize such 'wrong ideas' should they appear again. Thus the old peasants' stories become, in drama form, a model of a revolutionary attitude.

Fighting on the Plains, set in the anti-Japanese war, was written collectively by the China Peking Opera Company. Leading cadres, including Chiang Ch'ing, professional writers and the rank and file of the company took part. Chiang Ch'ing did the research and provided the company with the theme, historical setting and an outline of the heroic characters. She sent the production team to villages on the north China plain and other areas that had been resistance bases in the war, where they lived and worked with former resistance workers. From them they picked up various hints to give greater historical accuracy to the production.

If this seeking of inspiration from the masses smacks somewhat of romanticism or merely suggests professional thoroughness or, more likely, strikes one as a formality — it is now expected of all artists — probably a more useful exposure of drama workers to the views of ordinary people is from audiences who give their opinions while the play is in the tentative stage or even later.

The dancer, Mao Hui-fang, who plays Hsi-erh, the heroine of *The White-haired Girl*, in both stage and film versions by the China Dance Drama Company, wrote, 'I was brought up since the founding of New China and I have no experience of the sufferings of the old society. When we went to the countryside to perform for the peasants, they told me many stories of their cruel oppression at the hands of the landlords in the past, which deepened my sympathy for Hsi-erh and my hatred for her enemies.' One peasant told Mao Hui-fang, 'Hsi-erh was poor, she was used to a rough life. Why do you sway and totter when you show her wading across a stream?' Mao replied she was trying to convey the strength of the current, the difficulty of the crossing and thus the suffering of the girl. But that hardly satisfied the peasant who did not want the heroine 'to be so soft' Mao revised her steps.[19]

Unlike the professional companies, an amateur team works within a community of workers or peasants who are responsible for a part of industrial and agricultural production. Their performances reflect a familiarity with the relations of production and with social relations which the professionals cannot match. An examination of the evolution of the *Weavers' Dance*, produced by textile workers of Peking Vinylon Factory, shows the strength of the amateur teams in this respect.

In this short piece twelve girls dance to express their skill with the thread and their control over the machines, accompanied by lively music based on folk tunes. Songs punctuate and sum up their steps and gestures:

> Weaving bright clouds
> We shape the sky.

Finally they spread out the woven cloth in a dance reminiscent of both the traditional Peking opera scarf dance and the harvest dance of the north China peasants.

Most of the dancers were themselves from the factory's spinning and weaving shops. The music was written by the factory's storehouse keeper. 'We wanted to reflect the spirit of the workers,' wrote the team in the press in 1972. 'Our first idea was simply to go through all the motions of spinning and weaving as realistically as possible. As a result, the whole manufacturing process was brought on to the stage. But nothing stood out, the image of the textile workers was dim and all you noticed were the machines, no characters. The workers commented, "'It's only a dance of yarn and thread. You imitate the machines but where are the workers?"'

The team felt they had observed life in creating their dance but they had not yet 'concentrated, summarized and typified' the knowledge they had gained from that observation. 'Revolutionary art,' they concluded, 'does not mirror life passively but reflects it actively and consciously.'

They revised their dance so that it focused on the workers and relegated the operation of the machines to a subordinate position. To express the workers' feelings they found folk-dance movements insufficient and they turned to ballet for the steps needed. At the same time they interpolated the songs. The team showed the result to the factory's weavers for their comments. Next they performed it to the whole factory, then to neighbouring factories, revising it at each stage. Officials of the textile industry bureau selected the item to represent textile workers in the performances put on in the capital's parks to celebrate the twenty-third anniversary of the founding of the People's Republic, on 1 October 1972. The words and music of the songs were published in the national press and issued on a record. Professionals came to learn the dance.[20]

Similar successes in work-dances were achieved in the same year by rural drama teams. Tahsing County, near Peking, produced *Sunning Surplus Grain* based on the work movements of sunning, sieving, winnowing and sacking the grain and likewise using ballet steps to express 'the spirit animating the commune members.'[21]

The *Weavers' Dance* later turned up at a spectacular variety show given at the opening of a table-tennis tournament in the Capital Stadium, where its patronage by officials and professionals showed clearly in its slickness and loss of freshness and especially in a technical confusion which arose from a misunderstanding of a certain part of the work process. A machine operator is shown whirling on points down a line of girls each of whom represents a machine. The operator, in the original, 'switches' each machine on, starting a fast and realistic mime showing the passing of the yarn through the works. In the new version the 'machines' start working before the operator has even reached them. Evidently either the performers or the producers were not conversant with the meaning of the movements they were executing. It is revealing that when asked what the professionals had learnt from the Vinylon Factory's team, the amateur team leader replied, 'The spirit of the workers.' Yet most observers of the big dance companies would say that what is lacking in the professionals' stress on flair and effect is not 'spirit', which indeed, whether it is workers' or not, seems rather in excess, but a solid meaning invested in every step.

Hundreds of amateur items, however, by being less successful, escape the attentions of the professionals and officials and continue to have a local usefulness. The Vinylon Factory team itself had created scores of other items, ranging from folk dances to comic cross-talk and short operas, which were only played locally. A great many such items get no further than the factory that created them. Others do not go beyond the local amateur drama festivals: for example, 400 items were put on by nearly 10,000 amateur artists from 300 workplaces at a festival in the industrial city of Tientsin in spring 1974.

It is perhaps at the larger regional and national festivals that amateurs and professionals can best learn from each other. These festivals are held to promote on a larger scale a new development that began locally and at the same time to adjust local experiments to national guidelines. In 1963—64 a festival in Shanghai promoted a more proletarian style of modern drama. In 1964 came the festival of Peking operas on contemporary themes which, together with Chiang Ch'ing's speech at a forum during the festival, constituted the first act of the cultural revolution. More recently festivals in Peking in 1974—76 promoted the 'newly-emerged things' of the cultural revolution — in drama this meant adapting the revolutionary Peking operas to local forms, the renovation of *huachu* to bring it into line with criticisms made during the cultural revolution and the writing of new local operas on contemporary revolutionary themes.

The problems of creation described by the Vinylon Factory team are common to many drama groups and were a major topic of discussion at the forums at the recent festivals. There the companies summarized the experience of creating the model works, exchanged ideas on adapting the model works to other forms, discussed the creation of new dances and dramas and invited the festival audiences to criticize their productions. At the North China Drama Festival in January—February 1974, 1970 performances were presented over twenty-seven days to more than 230,000 people, over sixty per cent of whom were said to be workers, peasants and soldiers. Performances

Above: *Theatre as a working aid:* Weavers' Dance *by the amateur propaganda team of the Peking Vinylon Factory, celebrates the textile workers' mastery of their machines.* (pp. 64–5)

Below: *Party representative Ko Hsiang vows 'Marxism will save China, the Communist Party is the liberator of the workers and peasants' as she faces execution by the despotic landlord and his militia: the Peking Opera Company of Peking in* Azalea Mountain. (p. 104)

were given in villages, factories, mines and army barracks as well as theatres.

The key question under discussion is the portrayal of characters — how to typify from life in creating heroes. A meteorologist, Kao Hung, said that in writing the one-act play *Storm Warning* she restricted herself at first 'to depicting real events and real people. I had not raised the image of the heroine to a high enough plane .... The heroine must incorporate the strong points of all the first-rate people I was working with at the weather-station, yet not be entirely like any of them.'[22]

The Tahsing County amateur team handled the problem as follows. Their dancers had first tried imitating national minority dances but peasants said, 'You certainly jumped about and used a lot of energy but what were you trying to express?' So the team decided, 'First, the artist should choose themes from real life which are familiar to the masses and have certain educational significance. Second, dance movements should serve to depict proletarian heroes and the heroic masses. Third, there must be a correct relationship between learning from the life of the masses, which is the source of all art, and learning from the artistic heritage.' They now use previous successful works (ballets, *yangko* dances) to improve their technique — 'but we must not uncritically copy them.' The personnel contributing to the creation of a new dance make up a 'three-in-one combination' of amateur artists, local Party leadership and poor and lower-middle peasants.[23]

The problems of creation are more acute for professionals divorced from a context in the production process. The Tientsin Modern Drama Company wanted to write a *huachu* about middle schools. They fixed on one school and investigated the class struggle there. The result was realistic but hardly typical. 'To create an image of one, we must know hundreds. If we want to show the struggle in one middle school, we must know what's going on in several dozen.' Four years later they emerged with *In the Bloom of Youth*, a great success at the North China Drama Festival in early 1974, a play 'with great significance for the revolution in education', according to the newspaper *Kwangming Daily*.[24]

'A good theme alone does not make a good opera,' wrote Wang Shu-yüan, discussing *Azalea Mountain*. 'What kind of characters should be in the limelight?' From 1969 to 1976, all the model productions observed a strict rule regarding characters. This was the principle of 'the three prominences' or 'triple emphasis' — among all the characters, give prominence to the positive characters; among them, give prominence to the heroic characters; and among the heroic characters, give prominence to the principal hero. It was this emphasis on the positive, heroic and outstandingly heroic characters that provided a play with its educative function. Representing the good points of politically conscious workers and peasants in a 'concentrated, summarized and typified' form, the heroes were designed as models who would influence the conduct of the people.[25]

Indeed, the nature of the heroes, especially the principal heroes, is always held to be the key to what ideology dominates the stage. The nature of the ideology indicates what class is dominating the nation's culture. After the downfall of Chiang Ch'ing in October 1976, the theory of 'the triple emphasis' was refuted. According to *People's Daily* of 18 May 1977, it was 'a theory of creativity that caused works to distort life and become stereotypes.' The new 'correct' position is to create characters which 'truthfully reflect typical examples of the relations between classes in real life in thousands of ways and a variety of forms.'

Arguments over this question are at the basis of the last twenty-five years' shifting attitudes to the role of propaganda in the theatre — what forms of propaganda are appropriate to China's present stage of economic, social and political development? This intense concern with what is 'correct' for each stage of the revolution is perhaps the most outstanding characteristic of contemporary Chinese theatre.

Part Two

CHAPTER FOUR

The Plays of 1949–65

By means of land reform and the War of Liberation the Chinese Communist Party and people overthrew the corrupt and chaotic rule of the Kuomintang and the rural landlords and threw out the imperialists, among them the British and Americans. The war began in the countryside and came to an end in 1949 when the communists took the great cities. After years in which the country had been divided into areas under either Kuomintang or communist rule, with a shorter period when parts were occupied by the Japanese, China was now united into a centrally-administered state.

The United Front of the communists and the Kuomintang against the Japanese had been transformed during the War of Liberation into a United Front against the Kuomintang, composed of communists and democratic and progressive people, including many intellectuals who had previously supported the Kuomintang. These mainly bourgeois intellectuals had been impressed by Mao Tse-tung's appeal for 'New Democracy'. They had become bitterly disillusioned with the Kuomintang and were working to overthrow it. Many lived in the Kuomintang-controlled areas, suffered from censorship and persecution and organized underground propaganda against the Kuomintang authorities.

Liberation in 1949 was therefore first seen by many cultural workers as a merging of parts into a greater whole. With the unification of the country, the cultural traditions of the countryside would merge into a national culture under the leadership of the town and city. Writers of the old type, from the petty bourgeoisie, would merge with those of the new type from the workers and peasants, gradually eliminating the differences between them. Traditional operas would slowly be transformed into new-style operas. The foreign-style modern drama would merge with Chinese traditions to produce a national *huachu*. Urban professionals would ally with rural amateurs, give them sample performances and instruct them in techniques. Raising standards would go hand in hand with popularizing the new art forms.

Such harmony was not to be. Although conflict was muted by the need and desire for national unity in the years immediately after liberation when the economy had first to be restored and then put on a firm footing, divisions nevertheless existed in the ranks of the cultural workers from the very beginning.

When the First National Conference of Writers and Artists was held in Peking in July 1949, the 753 delegates (as many as 328 being drama workers) represented two forces — the tradition of struggle that had grown up in Yenan on the one hand, local, peasant-based, self-reliant, with a clear class perspective, seeing culture as an aspect of the armed mass revolutionary movement; and the very different revolutionary tradition that had evolved in the Kuomintang-controlled areas on the other, patriotic, national, led by intellectuals who saw culture as primarily self-expression. The two forces had already influenced each other. Yenan had absorbed many bourgeois intellectuals, who had journeyed there and taken up official posts in cultural organizations. Artists in the so-called 'White' areas had done much to further Communist Party interests underground and respected, and even admired, the social and political experiments taking place in Yenan. Now the two forces set about forming national organizations to weld a formal unity. The members of the National Association of Drama Workers, led by playwright Tien Han, and the National Association of Dancing-art Workers, both under the National Federation of Writers and Artists founded at the Conference, became the backbone of the drama companies that were set up in the following years.

Thus, built into the very structure of drama work in the New China, were two elements, reflecting two sets of experiences and increasingly two contradictory interests. The questions which arose and which had to be answered — whether to put the stress in forging a new drama on the professionals or the amateurs, the intellectual or the worker, technique or political activism, the city or the countryside, the Ministry of Culture or the grassroots drama troupes, the traditional or the modern, the foreign or the Chinese — were all questions directly related to economic and political policy, to the relative positions of agriculture and industry, leaders and led, Party and people, in the building of the new state. Finally they were questions of class. Which line of development would better serve the interests of the masses of the Chinese people, the workers and peasants? The development of drama from 1949 to 1965, despite its apparent harmony, was in fact a long process of clearing the decks for major struggles, of which we have already witnessed the first, the cultural revolution of 1966—69.

At the 1949 Conference, a Bureau for the Reform of Traditional Opera was set up under the Ministry of Culture, supported by leading artists of the Peking opera, Mei Lan-fang, Chou Hsin-fang, Cheng Yen-chiu and others. Veteran opera artists were retrained: in Peking alone there were over 1,000 undergoing these courses in 1949. In the liberated areas of the north-east before 1949, 200 traditional-style plays had already been written or revised. Local operas everywhere now began a similar process of reform. Texts were collected and written down. As many as 50,000 traditional opera scripts were said to have been collected in the first decade. Some were selected for performance, their feudal ideology was cut out, long plays were shortened and parts that were licentious or defamed the Chinese working class or peasant rebels were eliminated.

In a speech at the Conference, Premier Chou En-lai outlined the Party's policy towards the old art. He said old art was neither all good nor all bad. It should not be destroyed, neither should it be preserved intact. In another speech Chou Yang, who became deputy director of the Party's Propaganda Department under Lu Ting-yi, applied this policy to the traditional opera, which 'still commands a huge audience. It is an important legacy of Chinese national art. At the same time, it is a tool used by the old reactionary ruling class to deceive and drug the masses.' In the Yenan border region in 1944, among a population of one-and-a-half million, one million were illiterate and 2,000 were witch doctors. To show operas about goddesses to peasants steeped in witchcraft would not help them reduce infant or cattle mortality. Therefore, the revision of the old opera 'is an extremely important duty, involving a very complicated struggle of ideas.' It should not be banned but 'corrected step by step. We should realize that as the political consciousness of the masses increases, the liking for the old-style drama will diminish.'[26]

Fifty-eight old plays, so feudalistic they could not be revised, were in fact banned, while officials of the Ministry of Culture began to weed through the remainder. In 1951 a slogan was taken from Mao to guide this work, 'Let a hundred flowers bloom, weed through the old to let the new emerge', which was intended to refer particularly to the development of a variety of local opera styles. 'If old plays,' said Chou Yang in the same speech, 'are beneficial to the people by manifesting opposition to feudal oppression, corrupt officialdom, and by praising national integrity, public spirit, etc., they should be encouraged.' This remained the attitude of the Ministry towards opera reform over the next fifteen years. One of the reforms most welcomed by the majority of the people was the abolishing of the convention that the clown or fool was costumed and masked as a typical peasant, a custom that had long degraded the ordinary rural labourer. However, many feudal ideas continued to be propagated by presentation in the revised plays, especially Confucian ideas of filial piety and loyalty to the 'good' emperor, and the notion that there were officials in feudal China who had been 'good' to the people.

To demonstrate the effectiveness of the reform and to encourage its further development, a Festival of Traditional and Local Operas was held in Peking in 1952 at which 100 operas of twenty-three types were shown. In his speech concluding the festival, Chou Yang described the reform of the operas as a drawing together of the new type, represented by the musical drama *The White-haired Girl*, and the old opera, the latter 'gradually being reformed so that some of them actually differ very little from the new opera in their presentation of the new life.' The following year the Institute of Dramatic Research announced that sixty-three plays in the traditional repertory had been rearranged, fifteen either wholly or drastically reconstructed, and over 200 continued to be staged as before.

Writing in 1952 Mei Lan-fang gave examples of 'good old plays which we continue to value highly.' These included *The Fisherman's Revenge*, a story of labouring people's battle against tyranny; *Mu Lan in the Army*, depicting the patriotism of a Chinese Joan of Arc; *Fighting the Ch'in Intruders*, showing resistance to foreign invasion; *Liang Shan-po and Chu Ying-tai*, in which two young lovers rebel against the feudal marriage system; and *Meng Chiang Nu*, which protested against the forced conscription of labour used by emperors to build the Great Wall. He cited other plays that had been created by rearranging old ones and others still, like *The Drunken Concubine*, which needed only the excision of erotic, vulgar and similar elements regarded as harmful. Mei described how he gave up playing a banned play, one of his favourites, *Fei Chen-o and the Tiger General*, 'without the least feeling of regret.' In the past he had thought little about its content, being satisfied with bringing his performance in it to a high pitch of perfection which won great applause on his foreign tours. He had come to see the play's gross error, for it glorified a despot's lady-in-waiting who avenges her master by assassinating the leader of a peasant revolt.[27]

In local operas and especially in the musical dramas which developed from *yangko*, in modern drama and in amateur agitational sketches, much more progress was made in putting real characters, solving real problems in contemporary China, on to the stage. The musical drama, *Red Leaves River* by Yüan Chang-ching, was a vehicle of land reform propaganda popular in north China around 1949. Poor peasant Old Wang goes up into the mountains with his neighbours to reclaim wasteland. After years of strenuous clearance and terrace-building they build a village. The landlord, hearing of their initiative, decides to claim the mountain as his own and sends agents to extort rents from the poor settlers while he himself plays the charitable gentleman. Old Wang imagines it is the agents who are cruel and that if he could only speak to the landlord himself he would get relief. But this illusion is dispelled when the landlord rapes his daughter-in-law, outlaws his son for throwing a stone through the mansion window and destroys Wang's cottage. The daughter-in-law kills herself from grief, Wang's son escapes to join the mountain guerrillas and Old Wang, now a landless beggar, awaits his fate.

When William Hinton saw these scenes performed in Shansi in 1948 'the women around me wept openly and unashamedly. On every side, tears were coursing down their faces. Men wept too. It was as if the agony on the stage had unlocked a thousand painful memories, a bottomless reservoir of suffering that no-one could control.'

The second act showed the village after the Liberation Army had come. Land reform has been attempted but the landlord is still alive, 'still belching contentedly and still in control of the village,' praising Mao Tse-tung and befriending the village head. Then a county cadre, a poor peasant, comes to organize a Poor and Hired Peasants' League. The villagers receive him coldly, afraid to speak out, but at last he gains their confidence. The landlord is exposed and his land confiscated. A meeting is held to accuse him at which Old Wang's son rushes forward with a crowd of angry peasants to beat him. The cadre stops them and insists the landlord be handed over to the People's Court. The whole cast sings a final song of hope in the future. As the audience dispersed Hinton noted from their remarks that they preferred the second act to the first. 'They did not enjoy the tragedy. The pain it recreated was too acute, too close to their own bitter lives of such a short time ago. They preferred the optimistic final half, the battle and the victory.' But it had one fault, they thought: the landlord should have been beaten as 'the son-of-a-turtle deserved.'

The company performing the play, the Lucheng County Drama Corps, had fifty members, peasants who worked their land half the year and toured plays from harvest time until spring planting. They were paid millet tickets by the county government who also paid for their props and travel expenses. Performances were free. They moved to a new village each day and performed every afternoon and evening, lodging in village homes. 'This travelling troupe,' Hinton records, 'went in for realism. They provided a curtain, props, colourful scenery, and sound effects that included singing birds, croaking frogs, chirping crickets, pattering rain and howling wind. These radical innovations . . . were extremely popular . . . . People travelled for miles to see the performances and often followed the company through two or three villages.' In addition to full-length musical dramas, they played one-act comedies of the rural war and *kuai pan* items.[28]

Another musical drama of the period, *Heroine Liu Hu-lan*, praised a fourteen-year-old girl who was executed with a fodder-cutter by the Kuomintang for helping the communists. Others such as *Mobilization* and Fu To's *Wang Hsiu-luan* celebrated successes in agricultural and industrial production in the old liberated areas. Among the modern dramas, the Militant Drama Group's *Heroes of the Chiuku Mountains* lauded the People's Liberation Army, and *Struggle against Counter-struggle* was on problems of land reform, written by Li Chih-hua who became a stage director at the Youth Art Theatre in Peking in 1950.

One musical drama, *Everyone Is Happy* by Ma Chien-ling, dealt with the reform of loafers in the rural areas. Ma's previous *Bloody Tears of Vengeance* had been one of the most popular *yangko* plays of the anti-Japanese war, and one which Chou Yang praised for giving its theme of class struggle 'a strong, romantic colour.' *Everyone Is Happy* was one of a number of plays which showed the reform of people who had become delinquents during the breakdown and chaos of the Kuomintang rule. Another, *Gate Number 6*, a modern drama, told how Tientsin dockers smashed the gang system. Virtually a documentary, it showed exactly how the gangs worked; it took two nights to perform and was played by the dockers themselves. It was later shortened and included in the permanent repertory in Tientsin for several years. A similar play on prostitution in Peking was written by the girls themselves and performed by former prostitutes in the Peking People's Art Theatre. A play performed by a former band of Tientsin pickpockets exposed in detail their methods of training apprentices, thieving and disposing of the goods, against a realistic background of street and market life. The pickpockets proved born actors and their sleight-of-hand and ingenuity made the exposé a rather ambiguous success.

A more literary attempt to record one of the achievements of social regeneration, which at the same time spread public health propaganda, was *Dragon Beard Ditch* (1950) by the veteran novelist and dramatist Lao Sheh. The play revolves around the efforts of the new government to clean and rebuild the stinking ditch of the title, long a notorious landmark in a poor district of Peking. The characters are delineated according to their attitude to that major work of sanitation. It ends with a mad ballad singer offering his latest creation to a crowd of neighbours whose tumble-down dwellings lined the ditch:

> To all you people, I joyfully state,
> The People's Government is truly great.
> Is truly great, for it mended the Ditch,
> And took great pains for us, though we're not rich.

The growth of amateur theatre in the first decade was rapid and spectacular. Building on the network of rural troupes established in the pre-1949 liberated areas, the Party extended over the whole country its use of peasant drama as propaganda. By 1960 there were some 244,000 rural amateur dramatic troupes with a total of some seven million members, out of a population of over 600 million. In addition, there were some 39,000 amateur workers' troupes attached to factories and cultural palaces, run by trade unions and workers' clubs. Following the slogan 'Small in scale, rich in variety', the amateurs performed short operas, one-act plays, songs, dances and *chuyi*. They aimed, through entertainment, to instruct people in socialist values, assist current mass movements — such as land reform, campaigns against corruption, and the cooperatives — and, by praising model workers and peasants, to encourage production. The intention was also to raise the cultural level of the peasants by increasing their knowledge of state affairs and the international communist movement.

Documentary dramas soon left the past behind and offered more constructive help in building the new society. *The Gas Problem* (1955) told the story of Lu Wan-chun, an old worker who opposes the manager of a mine — a veteran revolutionary grown conservative — and enlists the help of an experienced engineer and the deputy manager in finding a way to rid the mine of gas. The play gave technical advice on eliminating gas in mines and putting natural gas to use. The documentary approach was also found in some musical dramas and local operas. *Building the North Chang Canal* (1959), a *laotzu* opera from Hopei, documented the hewing of a sixty-mile canal through the rocky Taihang Mountains. In song, verse and prose dialogue, it was written by the actors in collaboration with local audiences and showed the commune members' triumph over nature and over their own backward ideas during the Great Leap Forward.

The troupe responsible for *Building the North Chang Canal*, the Shehsien Hsiao Laotzu Company, was founded in 1952 by a group of village amateurs. 'We had no properties or costumes then,' the manager recalled, 'just a heap of old clothes.' In 1955 they turned professional but even then 'you could load everything on to a couple of donkeys.' Their plays dealt with personal matters — finding a wife, family quarrels — and they could handle neither bigger themes nor more ambitious spectacles such as acrobatics. They had no make-up 'and that was quite a drawback, for to begin with we had only men, all over thirty, even for the young heroine parts.' By 1959 they had recruited locally thirty-five women and girls and fifty men and boys and they could perform full-length operas. They won a prize at a regional drama festival and became well-known locally for combining labour in the fields and construction sites with play-acting, which was the company's principle in helping 'to change the face of the countryside.'[29]

But the documentary approach came under fire. When *The Gas Problem* was shown at the National Modern Drama Festival in Peking in spring 1956, it was criticized for its naturalism — 'more suited to a textbook' — and its faulty characterization. 'One could not quite understand why the director should be so opposed to pumping gas out of the mine,' wrote one critic, who believed the reason was the purely formular demands of the theme, conservatism versus progress.[30] Although the formular element in modern drama remains today, the tendency to naturalism has been replaced by a heroic approach consistent with the new stress on revolutionary romanticism.

The 1956 festival, held from 1 March to 5 April, brought together forty-one professional *huachu* companies from all over China. Four were from army units and two were trade union companies. Forty-nine plays were performed, dominated by those dealing with industrial construction. In this respect the festival was untypical of modern drama as a whole, since the amateur *huachu* of the time would mainly have been on rural themes. (Some 100,000 *huachu* troupes were said to have been set up by peasants and workers). Yet the range of its plays was wide. The heroine of the one-act play, *Liu Lien-yin*, a pretty young textile worker, convinces her fiancé that he was wrong to send an inexperienced worker from his record-breaking team to 'help' a rival team that has fallen behind in the race to increase production. In the comedy, *The Divided Heart*, a neighbour sees the co-op's storehouse keeper take a bag of fertilizer and assumes he is stealing it. She gets even by stealing one herself. Their mutual suspicions, one groundless and one quite justified, provide the humour. *You Can't Suppress It* and *The Waves* reflect the eagerness of poor peasants to form cooperatives even without the approval of the local officials.

Some of the contributions to the festival were by well-known authors, such as Tsao Yu, whose *Bright Skies*, written in 1954, won first prize. A satire, *The Imposter*, about a fake revolutionary who rose to high position by inventing a past for himself, was written by Lao Sheh. But most of the plays were by young or new writers, such as *Not that Road*, a one-act play on a rural theme by Li Chun, twenty-nine-year-old vice-chairman of an agricultural cooperative. *Home-coming* by Lu Yen-chou and *Household Affair* by Chen Kwei-chen, a woman worker, dealt with domestic problems, and they, in common with other plays of the period like the one-act comedy *The Women's Representative* (1953) by Sun Yu, showed women's emancipation in the new society. Other contributions came from the national minorities who brought plays in Chinese and in their own languages. Not all plays staged had topical stories. A number were set during the Long March and the wars against the Japanese and the Kuomintang.

In general, the difference between the festival plays and similar *huachu* shown today, apart from the recent abandonment of almost all love interest, is that later dramas interpret conflicts of character less as expressions of 'new' and 'old' thinking and more in terms of class. They stress the role of the principal proletarian hero who solves problems by reliance not, as in the plays of the fifties, on deputy managers, experienced engineers or trade union chairmen but on the ingenuity and perseverance of ordinary workers and peasants. However, there still exists today the division between *huachu* plays which serve as agitation, as active tools to shape the world, and those which see conflict in psychological terms and reduce class struggle to the remoulding of people's minds.

The recourse to the expert in the drama of the fifties, arising from a feeling that problems could best be resolved at the top, reflected the thinking of part of the Party leadership whose style of work was heavily influenced by the Soviet Russian way of organizing. This influence is felt in Hsia Yen's modern drama, *The Test* (1953), about two factory managers, one a bureaucrat, the other a dynamic elitist. The latter, the 'good' manager, 'together with the advanced workers, young technicians and experienced engineers, whom his lead stimulates, reorganizes the work and fulfils the plan.' Hsia Yen, a prominent author of social conscience dramas and patriotic war plays before liberation, became Vice-Minister of Culture and Vice-Chairman of the National Federation of Writers and Artists after 1949. A similar case was *Bright Skies* by Tsao Yu, author of the tragedies of bourgeois city life *Thunderstorm* (1933) and *Sunrise* (1935). His new play centred on efforts by the Party to capture the loyalties of the high professors of a U.S.-established medical college in Peking. The professors' difficulties in making 'a demarcation line between the enemy and themselves' and in starting 'to travel on the road to becoming people's scientists' were doubtless shared by the author. Tsao was director of the Peking People's Art Theatre and Vice-President of the Central Dramatic Institute.

Despite the rapid spread of the modern drama and its endorsement by the cultural leaders, there was still great difficulty in getting it accepted by the majority of ordinary people, for whom the traditional drama with its colourful costumes, songs and dances remained 'real' theatre and who asked, 'What kind of play is this, with actors in ordinary clothes talking among themselves instead of addressing us like in the old opera?' But others reflected, 'So village folk like us can be the subject of a play? That's new!' Coupled with a tendency which at times was strong to, in Lu Ting-yi's words, 'reject offhand' even what was good in the cultural heritage, the situation had by

1956 become one which defenders of tradition could exploit.

When in that year the policy of 'letting a hundred flowers bloom, a hundred schools of thought contend' was proclaimed for the arts and sciences, a number of old plays that had been banned were revived. One such Peking opera, *Ssu Lang Visits His Mother*, was shown in 1956 at Chungshan Park in Peking to an audience of 2—3,000. The play is set in the palace of the barbarian Empress Dowager, the camp of the Chinese Emperor's forces, and the military lines of both sides, between A.D. 976 and 997. It shows how the son of a Chinese general, captured by the barbarians, keeps his identity secret and marries a barbarian princess; when Chinese forces led by members of his own family attack the barbarian palace, he secretly goes one night to visit them, promising his wife to return at daybreak. After an emotional reunion, he keeps his word, parts sorrowfully from his family and rides back at dawn to find that the barbarian Empress has discovered his identity and orders his arrest and execution. When his wife pleads for him, the Empress relents and pardons him, but orders him to a post in virtual exile in the far north.

Previously regarded as unpatriotic, the play continued to be staged until 1960. In 1963 an article in *People's Daily* called its hero a traitor and his family spineless, and said that anyone admiring the scene of Ssu Lang's parting from his relatives was in a state where 'stinking fish smelt as fragrant as orchids.' Along with other 'poisonous operas' such as *A Visit to Hades*, it then disappeared again from the repertory, and plans mooted at the time for staging the erotic *The Dragon Flirts with the Phoenix* were abandoned. Another Peking opera of 1956, *Iron-faced and Unselfish*, showed Sung dynasty officials sharing out among themselves the taxes levied in aid of flood victims. At court the 'good' judge, Pao Kung, with the help of the emperor's uncle, foils them and restores justice.

Another 'good official' drama, the *kunchü* opera *Fifteen Strings of Cash*, perhaps the most acclaimed of the reformed local operas, was shown by the Chekiang Kunchü Company in Soochow dialect at the Tienchiao Theatre in Peking in May 1956, revised and shortened but not basically altered. The play, which first appeared in *kunchü* form in the seventeenth century, was defended in an essay by Chang Keng because Kuang Chung, the magistrate hero, 'appears as a good official ... who boldly stands up for the people and champions justice' and the play showed 'the high degree of courage needed to champion the oppressed in the old society.'[31] Certainly a line was drawn in the production between stupid and clear-sighted magistrates, but the histrionic interest centred on the comic clowning role of the cunning thief Lou the Rat, played in Peking by the veteran Soochow actor Wang Chuan-sung. In any event the notion of the 'good' feudal official was rejected just as the cultural revolution was about to begin, and so was the play.

Although 1956 was a peak year for the old drama, there was sharp conflict over the way the plays had been reassessed. The problem was discussed at the First National Drama Repertoire Conference in that year and there was intense debate around Kao Tse-cheng's fourteenth-century play *The Lute*. Did it propagate feudal morality or was it a realistic play of a popular nature? No conclusion was reached.

Summing up the Hundred Flowers movement in 1957, Mao gave stricter instructions on how to distinguish 'fragrant flowers' from 'poisonous weeds' in his speech *On the Correct Handling of Contradictions among the People*. The essence was the 'class character' of words and actions, which could be judged correct if they helped socialism forward, if they actively aided the work of social, revolutionary forces and did not oppose them or merely stand on the sidelines. Mao distinguished between two different types of contradiction in China's socialist society: those between the people and the enemy — imperialists, landlords, reactionaries — which could only be resolved through struggle, and those among the people themselves, which could be resolved through discussion. In future these guidelines were to apply not only to people in real life but also to characters represented on stage.

After this analysis of the place of culture in the new society had been published, and especially after the wide constructive upsurge of the Great Leap Forward of 1958—59 when masses of people mobilized to build canals and dams, develop steel production, erect factories and finally set up a system of agricultural people's communes all over the country, it became more and more difficult to oppose the growth of an activist, revolutionary drama equipped to help 'propel history forward'. Yet Lu Ting-yi and Chou Yang continued to lay the stress on gradually reforming the old opera. At one time in 1957 Peking was showing forty-two operas but only six modern dramas and two translations of Soviet plays. At the beginning of the Great Leap, in

June 1958, as part of the 700th anniversary celebrations of the life and work of 'the father of Chinese drama', Kuan Han-ching, about 1,500 professional drama companies throughout the country were staging Kuan's plays in over 100 dramatic styles. In 1960 plays on topical, rather than historical, themes were still in a minority of one to two.

The authorities sought to defend their positions. In *A Great Debate on the Literary Front* (1958) just before the Great Leap, Chou Yang recalled the early days of the revolutionary movement when intellectuals revered Ibsen's man — the individual, strong in his loneliness — and excused the slow pace of change by saying, 'Many of us embarked on the revolutionary path via the individualistic detour and joined the revolution with the individualistic knapsack on our back.' Lin Mo-han, a Vice-Minister of Culture, expressed it delicately, 'We intellectuals are connected with the bourgeoisie by thousands of gossamer strands' among which he numbered their friends or relatives, their education and their predilection for bourgeois culture which (and he quoted Gorky) was 'a mixture of honey and poison'.

Two years later, when Soviet experts, including drama advisers, were withdrawn and China embarked on the self-reliant course of political, social and economic development which it follows today, Chou Yang said, in *The Path of Socialist Literature and Art*, that 'Literature and art must serve the broad masses of labouring people and the great cause of socialism and communism.' But he went on to praise *The Runaway Maid*, *Over the Wall and Away on Horseback* and *The Pursuit of the Fish Fairy*. He seemed to suggest that literature should passively mirror socialist society and in the report, which covers seventy-four pages in English translation, there is no mention of literature and art as agitation, or of continuing the revolution under conditions of socialism, or of drama by the workers and peasants rather than for them.

Two *huachu* which successfully mirrored, but did little to propel, the great changes in the countryside after liberation were Hu Ko's *Locust Tree Village* and *Taming the Dragon and the Tiger* by Tuan Cheng-pin and Tu Shih-tsun, both produced in 1960. The first is a panorama in five acts covering events in a north China village in the years from 1947 to 1958. The first act, set in the land reform during the War of Liberation, opens with a slogan scrawled on the mud houses of the village, 'Beat Chiang Kai-shek at the Front and Pull out His Roots in the Rear.' It goes on to show the village Poor Peasants' League struggling to settle accounts with local landlord Tsui Lao-kun whose influence, through his son, reverberates throughout the play. The next three acts chart the progress of the village from 1953 to 1957 through the stages of mutual-aid teams and first- and second-stage agricultural producers' cooperatives. Act five shows the poor peasants, after overcoming inter-village rivalry and middle-peasant wavering, joining together in 1958 into a commune, a unit large enough to permit them to build a reservoir which will both store water and bring more land under irrigation.

Taming the Dragon and the Tiger, set during the Great Leap Forward, celebrates the efforts of peasants in a hilly forest district to tame the Dragon River by throwing a bridge across it so that the iron ore — 'the hundred treasures of Tiger Hill' on the opposite bank — may be mined and transported to support the national drive for steel production. In six scenes, each with its own title reminiscent of Peking opera — 'Glad Tidings in the Hills', 'Before the Rock', 'Advertising for Talent', 'Forcing a Crossing at the Devil's Gate', 'Together in a Swift Boat' and 'Sunshine After the Storm' — the play was described as being strongly national in character, yet its setting in the collective and its emotional exuberance recall the Five Year Plan literature of the Soviet Union in the early thirties. So, too, does *Locust Tree Village* resemble dramas of Soviet collectivization.

Though these plays certainly portrayed class struggle, they were not active agents of it and the struggle itself was still seen mainly as a conflict between 'backward' and 'advanced' thinking among China's masses. And if they depicted back-sliders among the Party cadres, there was no suggestion that the main struggle might be within the Party or that power-holders in the Party might themselves be the source of 'backward' thinking. Indeed, this possibility was unimaginable to many Party workers and it was with some shock that they heard Mao warn them in 1962 that it was within their own ranks that the danger of capitalist restoration lay. Although they had witnessed and deplored what they regarded as the revisionist course of the Soviet leadership in the late 1950s, few had countenanced the idea that a similar process had already taken place in the Chinese leadership. In 1967 a revised version of *Locust Tree Village* brought the play up until 1962. *Peking Review* then heralded it as the first modern drama to denounce Chinese revisionism and to focus on the question: Whither China — to socialism or to capitalism?

Amateur drama of the Great Leap Forward, however, came nearer fulfilling the activist function. Sketches, skits, songs and dances were played as a cultural impetus to the great work of changing the face of the country in the shortest possible time. The status of amateur and professional was temporarily levelled, or even reversed, as was to happen again in the cultural revolution. Professional troupes performed operas and modern dramas written by amateurs, schools were set up for a while to train amateurs, and training companies travelled through the rural counties instructing local enthusiasts. One professional skit from Hopei province, very much in the spirit of the amateurs, was *King Sweet Potato*, an item of pest control propaganda which, in a parody of the traditional opera, had all its characters, from Pest to Potato, using mask-like make-up, costumes and symbolism. The play culminated in an acrobatic battle in which all the pests were routed. The experience of the worker amateurs during the Great Leap was summed up at a national festival of amateur drama in Peking in May 1960, given by 2,700 performers.

In autumn 1962 Mao laid down what became 'the Party's basic line for the historical period of socialism' — 'There are still classes, class contradictions and class struggle, there is the struggle between the socialist road and the capitalist road, and there is the danger of capitalist restoration. We must recognize the protracted and complex nature of this struggle .... We must conduct socialist education.' Chou Yang, however, in 1930s style, continued to speak of literature and art serving 'all the people within the ranks of the united front, in which workers, peasants and soldiers form the main part.' (*In the Service of the Broadest Masses of the People*, 1962). The retort to Chou's line came in the cultural revolution: If in a socialist society the workers, peasants and soldiers form 'the main part', wrote Hung Chen in 1970, who forms the other part? The bourgeoisie. In a socialist society, what right has the bourgeoisie to a part in revolutionary culture? None. Hence Chou Yang, by supporting a culture for all the people and not for workers, peasants and soldiers whose society alone it was, had been propagating the culture of the bourgeoisie. United front policy, the critics reasserted, was not classless.[32]

Faced with this division in thinking in the cultural leadership,

Mao's supporters and opponents alike intensified their activities. Traditional operas continued to be staged, though the more feudalistic were again withdrawn. New Peking operas, using historical stories to reflect modern themes, were encouraged. Chiang Ch'ing, who was not known to have taken an active interest in drama since the Yenan days, began to seek another path. While she was not basically opposed to traditional or historical operas, she made it clear that they should be staged only on the condition that the main task for drama was not impeded — the task of staging dramas of contemporary life and creating images of workers, peasants and soldiers. She spent the summer of 1963 visiting and investigating theatres throughout the country, looking especially for operas which might be made into models of contemporary revolutionary themes. A number of Peking opera companies, such as that of Shanghai which began writing *Taking the Bandits' Stronghold* in 1958, had already experimented with contemporary themes. Chiang Ch'ing backed them but quickly came up against opposition from the cultural hierarchy. When she brought the Shanghai *huchu* opera *Sparks amid the Reeds*, the forerunner of *Shachiapang*, to Peking to be adapted into a Peking opera, rehearsals were frustrated by leaders of the Ministry of Culture for whom operas on contemporary themes were 'just like plain boiled water'. Boiled water is the Chinese poor man's substitute for tea.

Finding the way blocked, Mao summed up the situation of culture on 12 December 1963: 'The "dead" still dominate in many departments (of the cultural administration) .... As for drama, the problems are even more serious. The social and economic base has changed, but the arts as part of the super-structure, which serve this base, still remain a serious problem .... Is not it absurd that many Communists are enthusiastic about promoting feudal and capitalist art, but not socialist art?'

Chiang Ch'ing had found a measure of political support in Shanghai where the mayor, Ko Ch'ing-shih, in a speech on 1 January 1963, had urged local writers to 'Go all out to write about the thirteen years since liberation and eulogize the workers, peasants and soldiers!' Later that year Ko was instrumental in arranging the East China Modern Drama Festival, at which he made a significant speech.[33] In it he repeated Mao's point that cultural leaders paid lip-service to the line of literature and art serving the workers, peasants and soldiers but in practice they were 'cold and indifferent to dramatic art reflecting life and revolutionary struggle.' He charged them with saying that plays reflecting struggle were 'limited in themes', 'too simple and dry' and that the life of ordinary people was 'coarse', 'lacking in interest' and not worth portraying. Ko retorted, 'Only those who see with the eyes of aristocrats and lords regard workers, peasants and soldiers as "ignorant and coarse" and lacking in "fine and complex" feelings and thoughts. To the proletariat, it is the feelings of the exploiting classes which are crude and vulgar, corrupt and savage in the extreme.' He proposed leaving aside 'the emperors and kings, the generals and ministers, the scholars and beauties.' Furthermore, regarding the bourgeoisie, 'If we are to write about it at all, it is emphatically not to sing its praises but to expose it in the struggle we describe.'

Ko urged drama workers to 'go deep among the masses, into the heart of the struggle' and to 'break away from outmoded artistic concepts.' He advocated a reform far more fundamental than had so far been attempted in revising the old operas: 'To portray the workers, peasants and soldiers of today requires the introduction of their images, their language, manners and actions, that is, the introduction of new forms of expression which can hardly be found in the theatre of the past.' The careful rearrangement of old texts, the excision of undesirable matter and the writing of new operas on historical themes which constituted the main reforms up to then, was, in Ko's view, a defence of old forms. The real revolution in drama would come with the entire replacement of the 'set frames of artistic creation' by shapes arising from the demands of 'the actual life and struggles of the socialist era .... The conventions of traditional plays are suited to the portrayal of the ancients. Without proper reform they cannot satisfactorily depict the new people of today.'

The subject matter of the modern dramas at the East China Festival, held in Shanghai from 25 December 1963 to 22 January 1964, is indicated by the titles *Drought Fighters*, *After a Bumper Crop*, *At the Sales Counter* and *The Younger Generation*. A number of these plays were later adapted to other dramatic forms. An attempt was evidently being made to develop modern dramas as models of contemporary revolutionary themes for transfer to other forms; but it met two obstacles — the persistent attachment of ordinary people, especially peasants, to the old opera forms, and the resistance of cultural authorities in the 'stronghold' of the Ministry of Culture who did not think Peking opera was suited to material derived from *huachu*.

An uneasy compromise arose between the conservatives and the revolutionaries in 1963—64 with apparent agreement that all three kinds of opera (traditional, historical and contemporary) should be presented at the same time. The Festival of Peking Opera on Contemporary Themes, held in Peking in July 1964, while it was an embodiment of this compromise, did serve as a showcase for the revolutionaries' products. It was also the scene of the first open conflict in the capital over the policy for drama development. All three kinds of Peking opera were indeed to be found among the thirty-five productions staged there. The contemporary themes included the peasant uprisings of the 1920s, the Long March, the wars against Japan and the Kuomintang, the Korean War, the struggle of commune members against old landlord influence, problems of shopkeeping under socialism; and *A Bucket of Dung*, a long discussion between a man and a woman over whether a bucketful of nightsoil ought to be kept for their own plot or given to the commune.

It was in the speeches at the festival that the main differences between the protagonists surfaced. The conservatives appeared to take the position of their adversaries. Lu Ting-yi and Peng Chen, mayor of Peking, warned of the dangers of revisionism (the theory of 'the dying out' of class struggle) but neither defined what he meant by contemporary themes nor what relationship 'positive' and 'negative' characters should have in the new plays, while Lu said 'We are never against Peking opera staging good traditional plays or mythological plays such as *Uproar in Heaven* or *Monkey Sun Wu-kung Defeats the White-bone Ghost*.'

Chiang Ch'ing, in her speech on 5 July, asked 'Do we all look at (the revolution of Peking opera) the same way? I don't think we can say so just yet.'[34] And she gave guidelines in her speech for its development. 'Peking opera uses artistic exaggeration.... Therefore it is easy for (it) to portray negative characters.... It is very difficult to create positive characters, advanced revolutionary heroes.... Which side are you on?.... Our purpose in producing operas on contemporary revolutionary themes is mainly to exalt the positive characters.'

The most persuasive evidence of the imbalance in favour of the old on China's stage came in two sets of figures Chiang Ch'ing gave 'for your reference'. Out of the roughly 3,000 drama companies in the country, excluding amateur and spare-time troupes, about ninety were modern drama companies, eighty or so cultural troupes, and the rest, over 2,800, were companies staging various kinds of operas and balladry. As for the ninety modern drama companies, they did not all depict workers, peasants and soldiers, either, but laid stress on foreign plays and plays on ancient themes. Secondly, she pointed out that there were over 600 million workers, peasants and soldiers in China and 'only a handful' of landlords, rich peasants and bourgeois. 'Shall we serve this handful, or the 600 million? This question calls for consideration.'

Though Chiang Ch'ing had managed to get several of the operas that later became models staged at the festival she referred to this success only as 'the first campaign' in the battle to revolutionize Peking opera. The cultural authorities, on the other hand, seemed to consider the matter resolved, declared the event 'a great revolution on the cultural front', and had their speeches saying so distributed within weeks. Chiang Ch'ing's speech was not published until the 'stronghold' was overthrown in 1967.

During the period of the festival, on 27 June 1964, Mao made a further disturbing accusation: 'In the last fifteen years, these associations (among them, the Associations of Drama Workers and Dancing-art Workers set up in 1949) and by and large the people in them . . . have acted as high and mighty bureaucrats.' Mao attended performances at the festival, including, on 23 July, *Sparks amid the Reeds* by the Peking Opera Company of Peking, for which he afterwards suggested the new title *Shachiapang* This was the name of the village in the play whose lakeside reeds sheltered the wounded soldiers of the communist army from the Japanese marauders. He also said prominence should be given to armed struggle and the opera should end with the people's army fighting their way into the enemy's headquarters. He urged the company to strengthen the parts showing the relationship between the army and the people and to support the positive characters with musical effects and by improving their portrayal.

While Chiang Ch'ing and the revolutionary drama workers revised and experimented along the lines Mao laid down, the cultural authorities tried to undermine their work in private while in public propagating examples of their own attitude to the cultural legacy and its revolutionization, using not so much drama but mainly essays as their vehicle. The most contentious of the dramatic vehicles proved to be *Hai Jui Dismissed from Office*, a Peking opera on a historical theme, written by Wu Han, vice-mayor of Peking, and first produced in 1960. To Mao's displeasure, the play was clearly a defence of Marshal Peng Teh-huai, the architect after 1949 of a Russian-style army, who had criticized the Great Leap Forward and the communes and had been dismissed as Minister of Defence in 1959. While new plays on historical themes had legitimately satirized society under Kuomintang rule, such as Hsia Yen's *Sai Chin Hua* (1936) about a courtesan during the Boxer Rebellion, it was hardly intended that historical plays should covertly defend conservatives in a socialist society. *Hai Jui*'s continued acceptance by the Ministry of Culture in the early 1960s was seen by the revolutionaries as an attack on the 'Yenan spirit' in the army which, rejecting the Russian model and returning to the close soldier-people relations of the Yenan days, had revived after Marshal Peng's dismissal. Chiang Ch'ing had sent a statement to Hsia Yen in July 1962 reproving him for tolerating Wu's play. It had been ignored. But in November 1965 an article by Yao Wen-yuan was published in the Shanghai newspaper *Wen-Hui Pao* which criticized the play. For twenty days Peng Chen and the Peking propaganda apparatus prevented the article from being reprinted in the national press.

Divisions in the leadership that had existed since 1949 now reached breaking point. What was to become known as the Great Proletarian Cultural Revolution, simmering beneath the surface from 1960 to 1965, began in earnest in early 1966. In that struggle drama was to retain its position at the forefront of the cultural changes, reflecting in its crisis the much wider upheaval which shook the entire country's social, political and economic life.

CHAPTER FIVE

The Cultural Revolution in the Theatre, and After

The great Proletarian Cultural Revolution was an attempt by radicals, who enlisted the support of the masses of the people, to revolutionize the cultural and educational superstructure of the state and, in the Party's formulation, 'bring it into line with the socialist economic base.' The superstructure would then turn, it was argued, from one which had retarded development into one which helped to propel it. In the theatre, this meant an attempt to widen the area of agitation so that it embraced not only the short, activist sketches and propaganda items that already existed, especially in the amateur theatre, but occupied also the big stages and professional theatre, the biggest and most professional of which was Peking opera. At the same time the cultural revolution enormously multiplied the number of amateur and professional agitational teams and greatly increased both the amount of work they were doing and their status in China's growing new culture.

In the end the great majority of drama workers took the opportunity the cultural revolution gave them to reject their function of merely mirroring reality and began to grasp the theatre arts as tools in the radical transformation of society. And it was because it was in Peking opera that resistance to this tendency was strongest and because the transformation of such a highly complex art, which had grown out of an essentially passive feudal concept of man and life, presented the greatest obstacles to the would-be reformer, that the struggle there was hardest, most prolonged and most far-reaching.

A brief unsuccessful experiment had been made in 1958 to adapt the Yenan musical drama *The White-haired Girl* into a Peking opera. The play reappeared later as a model ballet but a major fault of early versions of it was a lack of revolutionary dynamic. The peasants in it were shown as passive images of suffering rather than as active agents of revolutionary struggle. Other Peking operas on modern themes had similar weaknesses. *Three Stones Street*, for instance, by the Peking Opera Company of Tientsin, chronicled child labour from 1870 to 1949 in the iron workshops in Tientsin Old Town, where the theatre was situated. The production, designed to illustrate a major exhibition on conditions in the old workshops being held in a converted temple nearby, had all the faults of a museum-like approach to the past.

What Chiang Ch'ing and the revolutionaries were looking for was something much more active and heroic: grand images of revolutionary ardour — realistic only in detail, romantic in expression, something elevating, nearer to the ideal — which could be acclaimed as broadly typical examples of proletarian virtues, embedded in plays that were easy to understand, colourful and attractive. There was a wide gap, however, between the desire and the execution. The revolutionaries had to go through a long period of experiment in the face of considerable opposition. The group within the Peking Opera Company of Shanghai responsible for the 1958 script of *Taking the Bandits' Stronghold* made little headway with it even after its performance as a revolutionary modern opera at the 1964 festival. There Mao saw and approved it on 17 July, but the authorities were still saying it was 'without much flavour of Peking opera.' They tried to remove the core of the opera — its political content — and proposed putting in some 'moving episodes' and 'startling scenes'. Chiang Ch'ing responded by telling the company, 'The play is sure to come out well. Be determined not to leave the front line until you win the battle!' [35]

The issue at stake was the portrayal of the positive characters. Chiang Ch'ing insisted they should 'stand out in sharp relief', and that the heroes must be proletarian. Further, in battle operas, which this was, the idea of people's war and the identity of the People's Liberation Army with the people must be brought out fully. The authorities said due weight must be given to the negative characters — the enemies of the people. They wanted the device of beating gongs and drums, traditionally used to greet the first appearance of a character of some power in the play, to be used when the villains entered. They tried to 'degrade the hero, Yang Tzu-jung', a scout in the P.L.A. In the play he kills a tiger, an act symbolic of his ability to kill the 'paper tigers', the bandit gang attached to the Kuomintang army whom he was fighting. But the authorities 'dragged him down to the level of Wu Sung, the individualist tiger-killer as described by feudal scholars in the old Peking opera *Wu Sung Kills a Tiger*.' And they said Yang, to deceive the bandits, should swear

Right: *Model hero, army scout Yang Tzu-jung, sings 'I'll melt the ice and snow with the sun that is in my heart':* Taking Tiger Mountain by Strategy, *Scene 8, by the Peking Opera Company of Shanghai.* (p. 82)

Below: *The principal hero 'completely overshadows the negative roles politically and morally': Yang dares the bandit gang in* Taking Tiger Mountain by Strategy. (p. 82)

and swagger just like one.

The revolutionaries retaliated by cutting out four negative roles and cutting down the stage business of the remainder. The bandits were made to swagger less and indeed to cringe before Yang, who was made to 'completely overshadow the negative roles politically and morally.' Chiang Ch'ing inserted a new scene to show Yang's closeness to the people in carrying out his military reconnaissance work. Extensive changes were made to music, singing, decor and lighting to support the new approach. In one of Yang's songs, at the words 'I'll melt the ice and snow with the sun that is in my heart', strains from the western-style tune *The East Is Red* were inserted to show that the sun was Chairman Mao. Although the audience was said to have applauded this sentiment, the authorities accused Chiang Ch'ing of abusing the art of Peking opera: 'The style of singing of Peking opera is sacred and inviolable.' Others said, 'Yours is foreign-style opera!' In another scene in a forest, powerful lighting cast brilliant rays of sunlight through the trees as Yang advanced. The complaint was that a forest is dark and 'these rays spoil the scene.' The revolutionaries retorted, 'What you forbid us to destroy, we will destroy! What you forbid us to establish, we will establish!'[36]

Between the 1967 version and the model script of 1969, there were 148 alterations to the printed text (English translation), ranging from changing the names of the 'black' characters (the impressive 'Eagle' becomes the less sympathetic 'Vulture' and the exciting and glamorous 'Big Pockmark' becomes the impersonal 'Bandit Chief of Staff') to replacing 'Neighbours, we are people's soldiers' with the greater class clarity of 'Neighbours, we are worker and peasant soldiers.' The 1969 script uses the title *Taking Tiger Mountain by Strategy* to throw the force of the title on to the positive idea, the strategy of the revolutionaries.

The Shanghai company had other, similar experiences. In 1963 Chiang Ch'ing saw a *huaichu* opera *Morning on the Docks*, the first play to describe the struggle of Shanghai's dockers in the years after liberation. She praised it for showing the dockers' 'courage and lofty ideals born of their internationalism and patriotism', and suggested that the company make it into a Peking opera. Work on it began in the spring of 1964 but the authorities objected that Peking opera was not suited to showing current struggles of the working class. Operas on industrial themes, they said, were too difficult to produce and 'If workers appear on stage, it will be hard for them to sing and dance in Peking opera style.' Then they 'suddenly became "enthusiastic"' and tried to appropriate the production. President Liu Shao-chi, who had headed the underground network in Shanghai in part of the pre-liberation period, saw the *huaichu* version and said that in his experience the dockers were not very selfless: 'When the Party raised a lot of money for striking dockers, some of them came up for the money twice, using false names. So we had to devise a check. Each docker was requested to present his carrying-pole as his identity.' He suggested stressing the theme 'bringing up successors', that is, depicting the real conditions and making the 'middle characters' central in the opera so as to show how they could be changed. But the revolutionaries regarded 'the real conditions' as 'the seamy side' which did not need stressing, and the 'middle characters' were waverers who could by no means be given emphasis at the expense of the positive characters, the dynamic force of the revolution. Nevertheless, a Liu-ist version was played up until March 1965 when Chiang Ch'ing saw it and pointed out that it distorted the original.

She immediately reorganized the group responsible for the opera (now called *On the Docks*), recast it and brought in new script-writers, whom she led. They rewrote the script, concentrating on 'creating images of Shanghai's advanced dockers emerging from actual life.' They made the play's woman secretary of the local Party branch, Fang Hai-chen, into the main character, supported by a worker, Kao Chih-yang, the leader of a loading team. Fang was given a complete song-cycle to express her 'lofty sentiments' and a series of melodies were written for Kao to show his 'straightforwardness, heroic calibre and high sense of political responsibility'. The theme of 'class struggle in the ideological field' was made to run through the whole opera. In recalling the old society, instead of emphasizing the sufferings the new opera 'fires the audience by the heroic struggles of the dockers in pre-liberation days.' Fang helps a young worker, Han Hsiao-chang, to see the importance of his work 'in the spirit of dedication to the world revolution'. Stress is laid on Mao's policies and Party leadership. 'The mood that gets across to the audience is one of militancy and daring, recalling the past ... but looking to the future.'

During the rewriting, the authorities 'sent their henchmen into the opera group to try to lead the script-writing astray' but 'their pens were seized.' When the new version appeared, they said it was 'devoid of artistic quality.' Fang's role was said to exist 'only as an advertisement for Party policy' and Kao was 'a dummy'. They said they would go through the opera sentence by sentence and discredit it. When it was shown over the National Day holiday in October 1966 they asked the group to reduce the number of performances, forbade foreign guests from being invited to see it and obstructed its performance before leading members of the Party's central committee. But Chiang Ch'ing advised the company, 'The oppressed people all over the world are longing to see our operas on revolutionary contemporary themes,' and urged them to persevere.[37]

By 1967, when *On the Docks* had won its place as a revolutionary model opera, the company claimed the victory as 'first and foremost a victory in the seizure of power' from the 'bourgeois cultural authorities'. The latest script, of January 1972, in the aftermath of the Lin Piao episode, stresses even more strongly the class struggle against the hidden counter-revolutionary, Chien Shou-wei, who 'tried to sell out his country' by sabotaging the dockers' efforts to load a grain ship destined for Africa before a storm delayed the sailing. Fang is now shown as 'good at seeing through those who pretend to support the revolution but actually oppose it', an obvious warning to the audience to beware of a second Lin Piao. Indeed, the struggle against Chien is now the chief dramatic conflict in the opera, relegating the conflict around the youth Han Hsiao-chang — a contradiction not between the people and the enemy but among the people themselves — to a secondary position.

If her struggle in Shanghai was tough, in Peking Chiang Ch'ing met with more difficulties. *The Red Lantern* had earlier appeared in the form of *huachu* and it was filmed as such under the title *Naturally There Will Be Successors*. In November 1963 Chiang Ch'ing asked the China Peking Opera Company to adapt a Shanghai opera version of the play to a Peking opera. Her instructions were to eulogize the proletarian hero Li Yu-ho, a railway switchman, in order to educate not only the Chinese but also foreign audiences — the opera deals with the Japanese occupation — in the truth that 'the political power of the proletariat is not easily won.' The authorities are said to have reacted this time by reducing Li Yu-ho's role and inflating the 'agony' of Li's daughter at the sight of her grandmother and father being tortured by Japanese military police. (This was also a criticism of the film which, according to an article in *China Recontructs* in 1973, made Li Yu-ho into 'a tippler drooling at the sight of his booze.') By dwelling on horror and suffering, 'they tried to upset and poison the audience with a touch of bourgeois sentimentality,' and the Japanese police chief Hatoyama was made the dominating personality. After Chiang Ch'ing's revisions, the emphasis was reversed and 'Li Yu-ho, given the best position and ample scope for movement, holds sway on the stage and gets the upper hand of the enemy.' Onstage torture was excised 'because we simply reject naturalism and sensationalism', and Li's execution takes place to the rousing strains of *The Internationale*. 'Anything detrimental to the characters of the revolutionaries — be it an episode, an aria, a sentence, a minor movement, or even a costume or make-up which was found to be a little out of place — was altered over and over again till it came up to the required standard.' The character of Li Yu-ho became 'a tremendous moral force "helping the masses to propel history forward"'.[38]

The first attempts at adapting the *huchu*, *Sparks amid the Reeds* to the Peking opera were done under the influence of the same authorities. The experimental version by the Peking Opera Company of Peking, *The Underground Liaison Agent*, even had a female impersonator play the title part, Sister Ah-ch'ing. In 1965 Chiang Ch'ing sent the whole company, script-writers and directors included, to camp by a reed-grown lake in Kiangsu province, where the play is set, to hear from local peasants and old partisans what hiding in the marshes during the Japanese occupation was like. They paid eight visits to army units to learn about the military history of the period and later visited the site of the concentration camp in Chungking run by the 'Sino-American Cooperative Organization', a joint venture of the United States and Chiang Kai-shek secret police during the War of Liberation. 'Such vivid education in class struggle,' wrote the company, 'made us understand much better the content of the opera,' After that they gave extra stress to the theme of armed struggle and people's war. The importance of Sister Ah-ch'ing in underground work was lessened, while the part played by the New Fourth Army platoon commander Kuo was expanded. They countered arguments that traditional Peking opera music was 'neutral' and could therefore be used just as effectively to portray proletarian as feudal heroes by saying, 'There is no music above classes.' The play achieved model status as *Shachiapang* in May 1965 and played 436 performances to a total of 655,000 people in a nine-month run in Shanghai, while Peng Chen, Mayor of Peking, commented, 'I don't see anything "model" about it!' He apparently resented the highlighting of the army at the expense of the underground. Today, playing in Peking, it is widely held to have the richest, and some say the most traditional, musical score of all the model operas.[39]

The last of the five model operas of 1964—70, *Raid on the White Tiger Regiment*, was developed by the Peking Opera Company of Shantung province whose early production of it was said by Chiang Ch'ing to be 'good on the whole but its generalization is not on a high enough plane.' There is a great deal of action and acrobatics in this story of Chinese volunteers in the War to resist American Aggression and aid Korea, and Chiang Ch'ing wanted it instead to give 'first place to politics.' The cultural authorities said 'It can only be counted as a semi-acrobatic type of play' and the Shantung provincial Party committee tried to exclude it from the company's repertory in favour of *New Wang Pao-chuan*, which 'extolled capitulation to the enemy'. They chose *Chiao Lung-piao*, which 'glorified a bandit' to be shown at the festival of Peking opera in Peking in 1964, at the same time attacking *Raid on the White Tiger Regiment* apparently to lessen its chances of being shown there. Peng Chen visited Shantung in May 1964 on an inspection tour and cancelled the performance of *Raid* half an hour before it was due to begin. He wanted to see the Shantung *luchu* operas *Bride in Her Sister's Place* and *The Change of Cave-house* instead. Mao saw *Raid* at the festival on 10 August 1964 and gave it his support and criticisms.

While the authorities ordered the Shantung troupe to abandon operas on contemporary themes since 'they don't show the quality of your company', Chiang Ch'ing drew up a plan for the revised version of *Raid.* Meanwhile the opera in its original state was filmed, 'a vicious trick, intended to standardize the version before it had been properly improved,' no doubt embarrassing the company in front of Chiang Ch'ing. She ordered the filming to stop. She set up a 'three-way combination' of leadership-masses-professional artists to revise the script 'by collective efforts as in a people's war' — 'rule by the voices of the many' instead of 'rule by the voice of one.' The authorities opposed this method and preferred to ask advice from 'well-known professors' and 'well-known experts'. They used material incentives — high salaries, royalties and awards — and the policy of 'three-famous' (famous writers, directors and actors) to 'win over and corrupt the younger generation (of artists) and make up successors to revisionist literature.' They spread the motto 'Eat well, sleep well, act well and have a good time' and 'prevented us from going to the countryside to integrate ourselves with the peasants.'[40]

The latest, September 1972 script was issued in a period of a more relaxed atmosphere towards negotiations with the United States, when diplomacy was once again seen as a weapon in revolutionary struggle. The 1967 claim was that the opera showed 'the U.S. imperialists' plot to deceive the people by continuing to fight (in Korea) while holding bogus peace talks.'[41] No such claim was made of the 1972 version. On the contrary, it supported the case that talks, such as then were taking place between China and the United States, were necessary.

Thus these long and complicated struggles to set up models of revolutionization in Peking opera reveal a pattern of sustained resistance by sections of the cultural hierarchy. The discovery and exposure of such resistance made it clear at what point an 'interest' in the literature of the past turned into a preference for it, and when a preference for it turned into actively pushing it, and when actively pushing it turned into trying by all means to subvert or prevent the rise of a drama which, aiding proletarian class struggle, attempted to show the heroic character of the proletariat in the age of the decline of capitalism.

Further evidence of the size of the task of overthrowing the 'stronghold' of Peking opera was the case of *Hai Jui Dismissed from Office*. Wu Han began writing this play soon after a conference of the Party central committee at Lushan in August 1959 at which Peng Tehhuai had spoken out against Mao and had been dismissed. Wu was known as a historian of the Ming dynasty and besides the play he published a number of articles, including one in June 1959, *Hai Jui Scolds the Emperor*. It seems that on the strength of these articles 'certain friends' approached him to make a Peking opera about the same historical figure, though Wu had never before written a play, still less an opera. With a show of modesty — 'I have no understanding of plays, I'm only a dilettante, far from an expert', — he agreed.

Hai Jui was governor of Nanking region in the Ming dynasty. He is recorded, says Wu, as having ordered the local oppressive gentry to return the property they had taken from the common people. He thus provoked the united opposition of the gentry, which led the Emperor to dismiss him from office with the accusation that he had terrorized and fleeced the people and oppressed the gentry. It is this incident in Hai Jui's life that Wu chose as the subject of his play.

In his introduction to the printed text Wu calls Hai Jui 'a famous, honest and good official' who 'would not submit to the fierce and overbearing' and as a result found that, though 'principled officials and young intelligentsia' supported him and 'the people of the period liked him and sang his praises', the powerful 'closed ranks against him'. Wu said his play was a 'brick' which, in the new spirit of the Great Leap Forward, he 'dared' to throw in order to 'stimulate the interest of my friends in the field of history.' And he concluded 'Hai Jui's position in history ought to be recognized. Some of his good actions and virtues also deserve our study today.' [42]

Peng Teh-huai had done or, it is said, wanted to do, most of what Wu attributed to Hai Jui, though not of course in matter of detail, and the play is generally accepted to have been a scholarly, rather clever and quite evident defence of the dismissed Marshal. But it is much more than an attempt at vindicating an individual leader whom a fifty-two-year-old scholar-official believed to have been wronged. If one reads 'Hai Jui' as Peng and the 'Emperor' as Mao, then the 'oppressive gentry' are the Party cadres and the 'usurpation of the property of the common people' is the setting up of the communes. While this reform naturally did not transfer the land to the private ownership of the Party in the classical sense, the communes certainly made vastly more effective the Party's administrative control of agricultural production and hence of the peasants. Seen in this light, the play is a calculated defence of the traditional forms of private land ownership — by landlords and peasants — against the new lords of the land with their communistic ideas. And it was in this light that the play's critics saw it.

Wu Han's use of historical allegory to defend conservatism was not an isolated occurrence. From 1959 to 1962 there was a strong undercurrent of such writing in essays, fables, stories, articles and a number of other historical dramas, both new texts and old ones revised. But Wu Han was Vice-Mayor of Peking, a non-Party member with some influence both in the Ministry of Culture and the Peking Municipal Party committee. He was thus a considerable minor figure in the upper ranks of the cultural hierarchy and the attack on him in November 1965 by the young Shanghai critic, Yao Wen-yüan, proved to be a convenient method of opening fire on very much more important figures entrenched within the Party, who, in the end, included Peng Chen, Chou Yang, Lu Ting-yi and the President of the Republic, Liu Shao-chi.

Yao charged Wu with using a historical story to attack socialism. Whereas Marxism, including Mao, states that it is the people who are the motive force in the making of history, Wu was setting up Hai Jui's honesty, the uprightness of a 'good' official ameliorating conditions under imperial tyranny, as a substitute for the people's struggles of the times. 'Wu wishes to replace the theory of class struggle with the theory of class harmony,' said Yao.[43] This was a major theme of the radicals throughout the cultural revolution. It was clearly stated in the *Summary* of the forum on the arts in the armed forces, held in Shanghai from 2 to 20 February 1966 under the leadership of Chiang Ch'ing.

The *Summary* declared that 'Since the founding of the People's Republic, literary and art circles have been under the dictatorship of a black line, a combination of bourgeois ideas on literature and art, modern revisionist ideas, and the literature and art of the 1930s (in the Kuomintang areas of China)'. The first step in combating this black line, the revolutionizing of Peking opera, 'will exert a profound and far-reaching influence.' Traditional skills had not been discarded irrationally: those which could be used to reflect present-day life had been retained and 'we need to refine, create and gradually develop and enrich the basic skills of Peking opera through our experience of real life.'

On creating model operas the *Summary* said, 'Only when we have successful experience in creating them will we be able to convince the people, to consolidate the positions we hold, and to knock the reactionaries' stick out of their hands. On this question, we should have a sense of pride and not of inferiority.' In particular, 'we must destroy the blind faith in what is known as the literature and art of the 1930s (in the Kuomintang areas of China),' and in the ideas of the nineteenth century Russian bourgeois literary critics such as Belinsky and Chernyshevsky and in the theatrical field, Stanislavsky.[44]

This was a blow against Chou Yang who admired these Russian authorities and who had cultivated the plays of the 1930s. The

Summary went on to repudiate Chou Yang's official Party slogan of the United Front of the late 1930s, 'For a literature of national defence', calling it a bourgeois one. Thereafter, throughout 1966 and 1967, Chou Yang, Hsia Yen and the other 1930s writers such as Tien Han, whose historical play *Hsieh Yao-huan* was called 'a big poisonous weed' by *People's Daily* in January 1966, came under increasingly severe attack which, indeed, in more generalized terms continues to this day.

After these authorities had been removed from office, the way became clear to occupy the 'stronghold'. To celebrate the twenty-fifth anniversary of Mao's *Talks* at the Yenan forum, eight 'revolutionary model theatrical works' were played in Peking in the summer of 1967: the Peking operas *Taking the Bandits' Stronghold*, *On the Docks*, *The Red Lantern*, *Shachiapang* and *Raid on the White Tiger Regiment*; the ballets *Red Detachment of Women* and *The White-haired Girl*; and the symphonic music *Shachiapang*. All other operas and almost all other plays were ousted from the Peking stage and these works became the staple fare of the capital's professional theatre for the next three years. The overthrow of the old opera and the growth of model operas was broadcast as an example of 'struggle - criticism - transformation' — struggle against, and overthrow of, the opera authorities, criticism and repudiation of their thinking, and transformation to a drama 'in correspondence with the socialist economic base.'

The same authorities had been the main supporters of *huachu*, and with their overthrow modern drama came temporarily to a halt. The radicals concentrated their fire in this sphere on the influence of Stanislavsky both on theatre training and on the writers of the older generation. The Shanghai Revolutionary Mass Criticism Writing Group undertook a study of Stanislavksy's 'Method' and published their analysis in 1969.[45]

The core of Stanislavsky's 'system' was taken to be the 'self'. 'The way to act is in yourself and only in yourself,' he said, and he advocated 'playing yourself all your life.' The Group replied: 'During the fifty-one years between 1877 and 1928, Stanislavsky played 106 roles, all of them tsarist generals, aristocrats, bourgeois elements or certain strata of townspeople' — all 'out of himself'. 'Can we proceed from the "self" of bourgeois intellectuals to portray the workers, peasants and soldiers? No. . . .' But when the slogan 'Combat self and defeat revisionism!' was used to criticize Stanislavsky 'those revisionist lords (of the Ministry of Culture) flew into a rage as if their ancestral graves had been desecrated.' The Group rejected the 'theory of germs' (Stanislavsky's idea that the self contains 'the germs of all the human vices and virtues') in favour of the theory of classes; rejected realism and naturalism in favour of a proletarian, revolutionary theatre of gesture, typification and class models, using dialectic to distinguish clearly the correct and the incorrect, showing, for instance, the arduousness and sacrifice of war but also its revolutionary optimism and purpose, showing the cruelty of war but not exaggerating or glorifying its horrors, depicting darkness and suffering but not so it predominated over the question of on which side is justice. Actors must not 'create subconsciously', as instructed by Stanislavsky, but must 'make propaganda consciously' while at the same time conducting the 'protracted, complicated and arduous process' of remoulding themselves in the service of the masses.

What may have been attempts by leftists to create model *huachu* alongside the model operas and ballets took place in Tientsin in 1967, when some students put on a play *Madman of the New Era*. The play was based on an incident in January 1967 when teachers of Tsinghua University in Peking raided a local mental asylum and released a certain Chen Li-ning who had been confined there on and off since 1963 for writing articles and letters criticizing Liu Shao-chi. The teachers obtained the support of two cultural revolution leaders, Wang Li and Chi Pen-yu, in publishing materials about the case, which the students used in their play. It was widely performed in the spring and summer of 1967, first in Tientsin at a Symposium of Representatives of Worker, Peasant and Soldier Literary and Art Fighters, then in Peking and all over north China. At the end of 1967 Wang Li and Chi Pen-yu were both attacked as 'ultra-"leftists"'. A Tientsin publication of March 1968 called the Symposium a 'counter-revolutionary black meeting' and denounced the play as an attack 'on the machinery of the proletarian dictatorship.'[46]

A more conventional attempt to create a model modern drama of heroic revolutionary fighters was *Chang Szu-teh*, put on in Peking in the autumn of 1967. A series of loosely related scenes retold the life history of the young soldier whom Mao praised, in a speech in his memory in 1944, for working 'entirely in the people's interests'. Chang was an example of certain virtues Mao and his supporters cherished. An incorruptible soldier from a poor peasant family who led a plain life, a guerrilla who nevertheless took part in productive work — Chang's army duties included charcoal-burning and it was due to the collapse of a kiln, and not in fighting, that he was killed — he was one of the model heroes promoted just before the cultural revolution whose pure devotion to the revolution influenced the Red Guards. This and other similar hero-dramas gradually diminished in popularity as the great upsurge of the cultural revolution passed its peak.

The upsurge was indeed immense. A nation-wide struggle to overthrow the constituted authorities of the state at all levels took place in 1966—68. Set off by the January Storm in Shanghai in 1967, the struggle released a great swell of creative ideas from the left, not all of them 'ultra' in tone. But as revolutionary committees began to take over from the old Party committees, the leftists were rebuffed and by 1969 the authority of the new committees rested on a combination of army officers, old cadres and some worker and peasant representatives. After 1969 the army contingents in the committees were progressively reduced and new Party committees gradually took over the work of the revolutionary committees in the following years.

The most widespread reflection in drama of the intense political struggles of 1966—68 was the great revival of agitational forms. Workers', soldiers' and students' groups travelled with musical instruments and the barest of props to perform propaganda sketches and dances at factories, communes, schools, universities and official buildings to give support to the struggle against the elite and in defence of the proletarian left. The movement marked the decline of the play as the property of the dramatist (performing rights, royalties, critical adulation, etc.) and the resumed rise of the play as the expression of a class engaged in struggle, created collectively and therefore anonymously and seldom published, the 'text' changing day by day and the form abbreviated and refined to meet the exact needs of an exact situation. It saw the further decline of the residue of the pre-1949 'star' system of actors and the further rise of the amateur cast and of children's agitational drama groups. Together with the model operas, the agitational forms were the most lasting contribution that the cultural revolution made to Chinese drama. They exist today, institutionalized and generalized in amateur propaganda teams, yet still potential weapons of political action in the cultural revolutions that Mao has forecast for the future.

Less lasting have been the song and dance dramas which, in 1966—68, celebrated in breathless melodrama the successes of the cultural revolution or, like *War Drums on the Equator*, the victories of world-wide people's war. Some rose quickly and fell as rapidly. The Chu Opera Company of Wuhan prefaced their performances of *Hundreds of Millions of People Follow Chairman Mao* in October 1966 with the announcement that they had taken 'seven days to make' their musical and 'eight days to correct it'.[47] It disappeared within weeks. Others took longer to research and were given more publicity. *The January Storm*, premiered in Shanghai in 1967, and *Spring Thunder in the South-west*, from Kweiyang in Kweichow province, were written and performed by 'proletarian revolutionaries who were victimized by, and struggled against, the bourgeois reactionary line' earlier in the cultural revolution. Their method of writing — collectively with the masses — was held up to the nation as exemplary.[48] It was certainly very different from the method employed by Wu Han who in writing *Hai Jui* had, he said, 'learned some things from my friends in the drama circle, some things from the specialists and some things from my non-specialist friends.'[49]

War Drums on the Equator (1966) praised the Congolese people for their victories in the war of national liberation. Its seven scenes show how the country's independence from Belgium, achieved in 1960, was followed by American imperialist penetration. An unemployed old worker, Mukania, and his family gradually realize the Americans have not come as friends, and 'take up arms to fight their national and class enemies.' With a list of characters including Congolese guerrillas, American G.Is. — both white and black — U.N. officials, a Belgian industrialist and soldiers of motley nationalities, the Chinese cast handled with some dexterity the obvious problems, though using only make-up and costumes, and not masks. They danced vigorously in bright robes and grass skirts to the beat of tom-toms. Backdrops of a modern city, rain forests, thatched huts and a U.N. camp set the scenes. The Epilogue has the cast of guerrillas advancing in a militant war-dance and singing 'Uhuru! Uhuru!' as a red sun rises behind the heavy palm trees by a tropical sea. The production, by the Drama Group of the Political Department of the Navy, was withdrawn as China's foreign policy changed to a more general support for Third World governments, as distinct from liberation movements. The Congo's General Mobutu, denounced in

Scene Seven as 'a traitorous bastard' who should be 'captured alive', was the guest of the Chinese government on state visits to Peking in 1973 and 1974.

As the high tide of the revolutionary movement receded in 1968—69 and the regional Peking opera companies got back to work, their first task was to present the model operas in provincial productions. This was part of the movement, which began in May 1970, to popularize the whole range of model works by reproducing them in a variety of forms including films of the stage productions, radio and TV broadcasts, gramophone records, posters, paintings, sculptures, children's picture books, postcards and even postage stamps. Their influence extended further into musical composition where use was made in concerts of, for instance, *The Red Lantern* in a version for piano with Peking opera singing. Excerpts from operas and ballets were taken to factories and communes where they were taught to worker and peasant amateurs.

Popularization spread widest when at first three, and later the other, model Peking operas were converted into local operas. Within three years about 100 local opera forms had been revived, mainly for this purpose. Even the Uighur opera of Sinkiang province, whose music has little in common with Han national styles, experimented with an adaptation of *The Red Lantern*. The principles followed in the revolutionization of local opera were said to be: remain faithful to the characters as portrayed in the Peking opera versions; remain faithful in style to local operas. The transition was not always easy. A debate in July—August 1971 in the Shanghai press centred on the *huaichu* version of *Shachiapang*. Actors and producers said that among their difficulties was how to use the wording of the originals without making it 'sound wrong' in Kiangsu dialect and with Kiangsu music. The solution was to change the wording but not so boldly as to change the meaning. Some letters in the press suggested the wording was still out of alignment with the requirements of *huaichu* but others praised the production's 'boldness in innovation'.

Considerable provincial activity had resumed in all spheres of theatre by 1972, when puppets, Little Red Soldier troupes, acrobats and modern dramas were already playing, local opera companies were beginning to write and produce their own new plays on contemporary struggles, and *yangko* dances and shadow puppets were showing in some areas. Local festivals were held in many provincial cities. In

1972 at festivals at Hofei in Anhwei province, and Hangchow in Chekiang, professional and amateur troupes showed a total of ninety-eight items, all new creations by local artists, including local operas, *huachu*, dance dramas, songs and dances and *chuyi* ballads. Acrobatic companies toured abroad.

After a series of experimental performances new productions began to appear in Peking. *Song of the Dragon River*, *Fighting on the Plains* and *Azalea Mountain* joined the existing five Peking operas as models, along with two ballets, *Ode to Yimeng* and *Children of the Grassland*. Counting the Peking opera versions of *Red Detachment of Women* as well as the ballet, and including the symphonic music *Shachiapang* and *Taking Tiger Mountain by Strategy*, the piano music *The Red Lantern*, and the piano concerto *The Yellow River*, the victorious cultural revolutionaries of the drama, still led by Chiang Ch'ing, claimed they had produced seventeen 'model revolutionary theatrical works' by May 1974.

The claim is significant since a criticism of the model works was their paucity. For five years there were only eight. Indeed, the upsurge of drama activity since 1972 has been a convenient cover for those who still oppose the predominance of the models. In late 1972 it is known that groups high in the Party leadership were campaigning for the revival of traditional operas. In 1973 a move was made to reject the model *The Red Lantern* in favour of earlier versions. In January 1974 the local Shansi opera *Three Ascents of Peach Mountain* was said to have been calculated to aid leaders who wanted to reverse the verdict on the deposed Liu Shao-chi. A struggle was evidently continuing in the new Ministry of Culture which was reconstituted in January 1975 under its minister Yu Hui-yung, a composer and former Peking opera singer.

In answer to the criticisms the success of the models was strongly reaffirmed in summer 1974 with a festival of the film versions. An article by Chu Lan, *A Decade of Revolution in Peking Opera*, reiterated their virtues. And the drama festivals in the capital in spring and autumn 1974 and further ones in 1975—76 were advertised as consolidating the gains of the cultural revolution by showing some of its fruits in Peking opera, local operas, *huachu*, songs, dance, *chuyi* and puppet theatre.

CHAPTER SIX

New Workers' and Peasants' Amateur Theatre

The amateur propaganda teams which flourish today were set up in 1968—69 on the basis of the much looser agitational teams of the cultural revolution. Being institutionalized, they came under much greater central control. Their task was to help the newly-established revolutionary committees in the factories, communes and other workplaces to rally the workers and peasants round them after a period of disunity and even fragmentation. They also helped to define what might be called the post-cultural revolution cultural norm, by praising the achievements of the cultural revolution and continuing criticism of the overthrown revisionists to undermine their influence still further. At the same time they were expected to revive the pre-cultural revolution duties of amateur teams — to support current campaigns and mass movements, to propagate the general ideas of socialism and to inspire people with a consciousness and confidence to work hard and well. This last function, the use of theatre as a working aid, is perhaps the amateur teams' most fundamental duty today. Their entire aims, however, may be summed up in Mao's definition of the purposes of propaganda: 'To organize, to stimulate, to agitate, to criticize, to propel.'

The means the teams adopt in every case is to present a model of conduct in dramatic form. The plots should not merely illustrate. As in the case of the model works but in a more down-to-earth way, they must in simple, dialectical form show contradictions in the act of resolution. Even a short item, like *Shoes to Strike Roots*, by the amateur propaganda team of Tahsing County, may encompass an elementary dialectic. This ten-minute dance provides a reminder of a tradition of the revolutionary wars when village women showed their support for the red soldiers by sewing cloth shoes for them out of pieces of rag. Today, when boys and girls leave middle school, many of them go to settle in the countryside. These 'educated youth' and the peasants, from such different backgrounds, constitute a unity of opposites. While the youth are anxious as to how the peasants will receive them, the peasants wonder how the inexperienced young will adapt to the different life. The humble cloth shoe is the agent of the resolution of this contradiction. The peasant women, carrying on the tradition, make cloth shoes for the youth. The youth are moved. They want to know how to make them themselves. Then follows a dance with mime, based partly on *yangko*, in which the young people learn the skill from the old women. Having succeeded in this, the young people face the next task in 'striking roots in the countryside' with the confidence of a raised consciousness. A new unity of opposites springs up, new contradictions arising from the new task will have to be resolved.

Any familiar and typical stage in the development of rural and industrial life may be taken as raw material. *Shoes to Strike Roots* supported the rural resettlement programme of the urban youth. The amateur team of the Sanlien Production Brigade in Kwangsi province spent 1968—70 producing items in support of the peasants' Marxist-Leninist study programme. They also wrote an opera about the campaign to train 'barefoot' doctors who began treating minor complaints in the villages during the cultural revolution.

A recurring campaign is one which contrasts the present with the past. The team attached to Chenshan Brigade, Huangshan Commune, Chekiang province, composed a cross-talk *New Look of Chenshan Brigade*, which traced progress in irrigation, from manually-operated and animal-drawn waterwheels before liberation to power-driven wells today. A ballad, *A World of Difference*, compared the drought of 1926 in the area, which drove 110 of the 250 families out of the village to wander into towns, go begging and sell their children, with a drought in 1972 when the brigade reaped record harvests of cotton and grain.

In Kweichow province, the Bamboo Basket Theatrical Troupe staged a local opera on the peasants' past misery when they lived in rags and ate wild vegetables. A troupe of the Pashe Production Brigade in Kwangtung province composed 173 items between 1968 and 1972 including *Pashe, Today and Yesterday*, which helped 'commune members recall the bitter past and portrays today's happy life, thus adding to their revolutionary enthusiasm.' A housewife in Chinshan, near Shanghai, performed a story *Reunion of Mother and Daughter* at a Home for the Aged in a neighbouring commune. The story told how mother and daughter, driven apart by poverty before liberation, were reunited afterwards. Young amateurs of Kaisung Commune in Tibet wrote a *huachu*, *Three Generations*, about a family of slaves, and played it to audiences of emancipated slaves and serfs. It showed the family fighting against its bondage.

In the Pearl River delta in the far south, twenty former housewives in Chiangmen city, now working in local workshops, set up a Mothers' Cultural Group in 1971. The idea came from a sailor's wife, Kuo Shao-ping, who, when she saw her neighbours attending politics classes at evening school, reflected upon discrimination against women in the old society. One of their items showed the selling of women into concubinage and service for the rich in pre-liberation China. Another item praised some housewives who, no longer bound by household chores, work in the small neighbourhood factories set up during the cultural revolution. The group tours neighbourhoods, cultural centres, factories and nearby communes.

When the campaign to criticize Confucius joined with the posthumous repudiation of Lin Piao to produce a nationwide critical movement in early 1974, the propaganda teams in the countryside around Shanghai, a traditional centre of the story-telling art where nearly a million story-tellers are active today, wrote hundreds of stories on this theme alone. One nineteen-year-old middle school leaver wrote *Tear up the Sinister Restorationist Flag*, a criticism of lingering revisionism, and *The Careerist Instructs His Son to Revere Confucius and Study the Confucian Classics*, an onslaught on Lin Piao who is said to have done just that. She recites her stories in full, on threshing grounds, in commune-run workshops and at evening schools to audiences as large as 8,000.

Some items support long-term land improvement projects. Wanwei Island, off the south China coast, has a thirty-four-member team for its 2,000 inhabitants. It composed ninety songs, dances and short plays between 1968 and 1973. A *huachu* by the team records their success in reclaiming land from the sea, and a song and dance drama, *The Island Detachment of Women*, shows the women militia's work in reclamation, farming, and military training. The Tahsing County troupe's *Red Flowers on Dry Land* is a dance praising the peasants' revolutionary spirit in conquering drought.

Other items support campaigns that have a more direct relation to production. When the Kangkeng Brigade of an east Fukien commune was popularizing improved strains of seed in 1970, the brigade's team put on a one-act play *Praise Good Strains of Seed*. Output doubled the next year. *Model Pig-raisers* and *Nursing Seedlings*, by the

Tahsing team, are dances that act similarly as working aids, praising good work methods. The Yao and Chuang minorities of south-west China have eliminated superstitious elements in their dances and use traditional folk tunes with new content. The Yao's *The Hungfeng No. 1 Is Sent to Peking* is a copper-drum dance celebrating the development by local peasants of a new strain of high-yield maize.

Other pieces praise individuals for their socialist spirit. The Chenshan Brigade's team in Chekiang wrote a clapper-ballad about a sixty-one-year-old storehouse keeper who saved 250 kilogrammes of grain from dust swept off the threshing ground of his production team during the early rice harvest. All the village was asked to emulate his example and as a result the brigade retrieved 1.1 tons of grain.

The Tahsing team's *Story of Wang*, a *tan hsien* performed by seven girls in red tops, light blue trousers and cloth sandals, recounts the true struggle of another folk hero, Wang Kuo-fu, a production brigade leader in a formerly abjectly poor area north of Peking. After liberation Wang chose not to have a special house just because he had been elected a village leader but instead lived in a one-room shack as he had done when a poor peasant, calling it Hired-hand Room to remind him of his past. In the *tan hsien* the peasants praise him for staying 'with the people' but one Liu Lao-ssu criticizes him, seeking Wang's job with the aim of being promoted. When the commune wins a good harvest, Liu tries to win support for himself by suggesting the villagers keep most of it and sit back and eat, selling less to the state to feed the cities or to be stored against hard times. The villagers debate this and accuse Liu of waste. Then another official, Hu Peng, is sent to the village by higher leaders and orders Wang's dismissal, proposing Liu as brigade leader in his place. But the villagers vote for Wang. 'If a few gain now,' says Wang, 'many will not gain in the end. Let us eat and be healthy, certainly, but I will remain an ox pulling the revolutionary cart.'

A number of items deal with education. A drum-ballad, *Sending a Daughter to University*, sung in dialect by a Tientsin printing worker, celebrated the reform of the educational system, which, since the cultural revolution, has admitted more worker and peasant children into higher learning. Some of the school leavers who settle in the countryside form their own teams. In the north eastern province of Heilungkiang, whose marshy wastelands 900,000 resettled youth are helping to open up, an eight-day amateur theatrical festival was held in the summer of 1974. One hundred and thirty-two items were presented — excerpts from model operas, plays, songs and dances and instrumental pieces. Young tractor drivers, cooks and herdsmen put on the ballet *The White-haired Girl*. Two school-leavers wrote a short play about breeding new varieties of soya bean, a basic crop in the north-east. Others composed ballads in local styles showing their attempts to settle in the virgin land.

While schools and city districts have Little Red Guard troupes of children, in some places old people have got together and gone on stage. In Shenyang city, a Grandmothers' Choral Club sings well-known arias from the model Peking operas. The choir has thirty-three members, with an average age of sixty, the oldest being seventy-eight. In celebration of the Party's fifty-third anniversary on 1 July 1974 they performed at a concert on a sports field in the city before an audience of 10,000. In four years these retired working women gave 183 performances at local meetings, in schools, factories, army units, offices, theatres and parks.

Of the very great number of amateur teams in the factories, those belonging to the Vinylon Factory and the Capital Iron and Steel Works are well-known in Peking. The steel workers' *Tapping Molten Steel* and *Flames of the Furnace Are Fiery* are dances which generate a feeling of excitement in gigantic industrial processes which have been turned to the people's benefit.

The Vinylon team, apart from its *Weavers' Dance*, has a lively *kuai pan*, *The New Painter*. Written by a maintenance worker, it tells the true story of a young man who was assigned to the factory as a trainee house painter. He fears dirtying his hands, but when his old master tells him to paint the gate of the factory and he falls off the ladder spilling two pots of paint, he sees the master scoop up the spilt paint with his hands rather than see it wasted. The next test, painting the walls of a toilet, appeals to the trainee even less. In any case, the job is too simple, he thinks. But when he has finished it, the workers criticize him for laying on the paint too thickly — if it's so simple, why did he do it wrong, they ask him? The third stage of transition to conscientiousness is when he is asked to paint the insides of the huge automatic machines which clean the vinylon material. These reek of formaldehyde, are stuffy and dark, and are entered only by a small hatch. The inside must not get rusty: this is real painting, he thinks. He gets inside the machine with his paint pot and brush and emerges a hero.

The No. 4 State Cotton Mill in Tientsin has a *Weavers' Dance* and a variety of other items. A song with actions and gestures, *Patching Gloves*, shows three veteran workers repairing worn-out gloves. 'Why mend old ones when we have plenty of new ones?' some girl apprentices ask. 'Extravagance is a bourgeois habit,' comes the reply. *In Praise of the Secretary*, a *piao yen chang*, is based on incidents in the life of a textile worker who is a workshop Party secretary known for her conscientious study of politics. A *kuai pan* praises a master worker in the mill's weaving shop who, despite the fact he is beyond retiring age, keeps on at his job. Skits, drum-ballads and excerpts from Peking operas are among the eighty pieces the mill produced in the four years from 1968. Eight hundred amateurs took a direct part in the writing and staging.

Through participation in amateur teams, disabled workers are encouraged to contribute to cultural life. At Tientsin's Chungkuang Hardware Factory for the Blind, blind and disabled workers and deaf-mutes set up a propaganda team. Led by the blind vice-chairman of the factory's revolutionary committee, they perform a wide variety of dances, songs and conjuring tricks.

Not all amateur drama is short. The amateur teams attached to government bureaux, industrial organizations and army units attempt longer works in the *huachu* form. In 1973 the Railway Bureau's team, for example, put on an adaptation of Hao Jan's novel *Bright Sunny Skies* which lasted nearly four hours. A number of these longer modern dramas appear at the regional drama festivals.

CHAPTER SEVEN

New Professional Productions

Major activity in Peking's professional theatre between 1970 and 1974 centred on the cultivation of new model works. Among them were the Peking opera *Azalea Mountain* and the ballet *Ode to Yimeng*.

Azalea Mountain is set in 1928, one year after Mao Tse-tung and his followers set up the first revolutionary base in the Chingkang Mountains. It was then that Mao began to evolve a strategy for the revolution: building revolutionary bases and surrounding, and finally seizing, the cities. In the play, peasants in the area, inspired by recent communist-led uprisings, have set up a Self-defence Corps, and a Party worker, Ko Hsiang, has been sent to establish contact with them. The Corps is demoralized after suffering three defeats at the hands of the landlord militia. When they hear Ko has been arrested on her way to find them, they organize her rescue just as she is about to be executed. The Corps accepts Ko as their Party representative and she starts to transform them from a desperate bandit gang into conscious revolutionary fighters. She trains their leader, Lei Kang, a boisterous peasant, to distinguish friend from enemy. The Corps attacks the local despot's mansion, distributes his grain among the local people and wins new recruits. The Corps sets up headquarters on Azalea Mountain but the landlord militia blockades it and holds Lei Kang's foster-mother as hostage down in the village. By using a renegade inside the Corps, the landlord tricks Lei Kang into descending to the village where he is caught. Ko, angry at Lei's impetuous action, nevertheless takes a rescue party along precipitous mountain paths in a torrential rainstorm and after a stylized scene of mime, somersaults, splits, springs, vaults and leaps, they reach the village, shoot the guards and snatch away Lei and his foster-mother. Meanwhile, on the mountain, the renegade has tried to make the remainder of the demoralized Corps surrender but Ko, arriving back in time, kills him and spells out the lesson Lei must learn. 'Do not be deceived by false "comrades",' she says. And in a final aria in what amounts to an elegy on the Lin Piao conspiracy, she addresses the people:

> Why having smashed your chains were you chained again?

Why did you close your ears to the truth
And let blatant lies deceive you?
It was narrow loyalty and longing for vengeance
That blinded you to the long, long road
We must take to make revolution.
For generations slaves have fought for freedom,
But lacking a clear aim these rebels lost their bearings;
Countless heroes died in vain, cursing heaven high.
The peasants' armed forces must keep close to the Party,
The Party commands the gun.

Chastened, the Corps 'like a stream flowing into the sea' joins with units of the Workers' and Peasants' Revolutionary Army and together they kill the local despot in a final outburst of acrobatics. Triumphantly the Corps marches off to the Chingkang Mountains to be incorporated into Mao's forces.

The opera, in nine scenes and rhymed dialogue, creates in Ko Hsiang 'the heroic image of a Party political worker handling intense and complicated contradictions, a capable leader close to the day-to-day problems of the masses, yet far-sighted', and in Lei Kang 'a hero who develops from a peasant in spontaneous struggle, daring to rebel and undaunted by obstacles, into a conscious and disciplined proletarian fighter.'[50] An earlier version of the opera appeared before the cultural revolution. The new production, by the Peking Opera Company of Peking, spent two years in an experimental form before being declared a model in September 1973. It toured Algeria in 1974 and a film of it has been shown widely in China and abroad.

The ballet, *Ode to Yimeng*, emerged at the same time, after a similar period of experimentation. In a prologue, four acts and an epilogue, the production by the China Dance Drama Company at Peking's Tienchiao Theatre celebrates the unity of the army and the people in the War of Liberation. After a battle a P.L.A. platoon commander, Fang, lies wounded and unconscious on a mountain slope. Both Kuomintang troops and some local villagers who support the communists are trying to find him. A villager, Sister Ying, goes up the mountain to seek wild vegetables and comes across the wounded soldier. She finds Fang's water bottle is empty. She is too far from the village to go for water, so she takes the bottle and going behind a rock fills it with her own milk. As a violin sobs with emotion, she props Fang up and feeds him the milk from the bottle. He recovers and, moved, rises and salutes her. Enemy soldiers approach and while Fang hides, Sister Ying goes home and kills a chicken to make some soup for him. That night the enemy raid the village, searching for Fang. Breaking into Sister Ying's house they see the soup and suspect it is for Fang. They threaten Sister Ying who denounces them sternly. They beat her and torture her until she falls unconscious. When she recovers they plan to follow her but she escapes through a rear window with the soup. Meanwhile her husband has mustered an armed team to rescue Fang. Meeting Sister Ying on the mountain the enemy soldiers threaten to kill her baby if she will not reveal where Fang is, but Fang breaks out of hiding and stops them. At that moment, her husband and the team rush in and kill the enemy. The epilogue shows Fang marching off to return to his platoon, 'taking the villagers' deep friendship and profound love with him.'

The same theme is treated in the short dance drama *Like Fish and Water* by the Cultural Troupe of the Political Department of the P.L.A. Railway Corps. It tells the story of a unit of P.L.A. soldiers who come to a mountain village during manoeuvres. They are welcomed by the village women with a red scarf dance. Although they are tired after long marching, the soldiers go off to help pick the villagers' apples. One soldier finds his cloth shoes are worn out. The peasant with whom he is billeted wants secretly to make him a new pair. But as she does not know his measurements, the other villagers suggest she should sweep the path clean just before the soldier goes to the well to fetch water for her. From his footprints on the path she finds out the size of his feet and she makes the shoes that same night. Meanwhile the soldier, in trying to carry more than two buckets from the well at once, breaks the woman's carrying pole and he decides to make her a new one that night.

The central scene shows the soldier sitting in moonlight on one side of the stage whittling a new pole, while on the other the peasant woman sits inside her cottage carefully stitching a pair of shoes, each unknown to the other. At dawn the unit marches off and half way up the hill the soldier discovers the new shoes in his pack. Fondly he looks back at the village. Meanwhile the villagers find the new carrying pole and gaze with affection after the departing soldiers. Represented on stage at the same time, these two groups of people, spatially separated but joined in solidarity, form a final tableau underlining the common saying that 'the people's soldiers move among the people like fish in water.' Using a basis of ballet steps, the piece makes considerable use of Chinese folk dance movements. Chinese traditional instruments are introduced into the western-style orchestra and the music is based on folk tunes. Two songs are incorporated, one in the moonlit scene and the other as a finale.

Another major work showing in the capital, of rather a different kind, was *Hsiangyang Store* (or *The Shop Facing the Sun*), a *pingchu* opera about class struggle in the Peking retail trade. The story takes place in a store in the industrial suburbs where nineteen-year-old Liu Chun-hsiu works as an assistant. When she sees an old worker coming in from an outlying housing estate to buy goods for his mates at work, she proposes to the management to start up a mobile shop. The store's Party branch secretary Wang agrees and offers to push the cart. Manager Liu, Chun-hsiu's father, does not think it will bring in much money but reluctantly accepts the proposal.

Pan, an ex-capitalist, who is the buyer for the store, has been selling stocks illegally to the estate at higher prices and thinks that the mobile sellers will discover this. He tries to dissuade them from going but Chun-hsiu and Wang set off with their home-made, brightly-painted cart which runs on two bicycle wheels. Pan conspires with a profiteer on the estate and sabotages the cart by removing a nut, causing it to tip over, injuring Chun-hsiu and damaging the cart.

Prodded by Pan, Manager Liu angrily denounces the scheme as worthless, but Chun-hsiu persists, selling goods from a basket on her back. Her efforts are supported by the people on the housing estate but Liu is furious and demands that she asks for a transfer to another store. Wang, played by the famous *pingchu* actor Ma Tai, in a long duet with Liu reminds him of their past together selling goods for the peasants in the liberated areas before 1949 and insists that Chun-hsiu is good and is carrying on the tradition. Liu relents and agrees to investigating Pan. An inventory is taken of the stock. Desperate, Pan breaks into the accountant's office at night to steal the books. Chun-hsiu surprises him and they struggle. Pan nearly kills her but Wang and some workers rush in and catch him. In the last of the eight scenes, titled 'New Starting Point', customers express their thanks for good service and the opera ends with a song and dance praising Mao's concept of 'Serve the people', and a vow to make the shop 'turn full-face to the sun.'

The writers and cast of the Peking Pingchu Company worked in over forty stores in three provinces and four cities while creating the opera, serving customers, pushing carts, delivering to the people's houses and packing goods. Many of the humorous touches in the dialogue and arias are taken from their experience. The opera first appeared in 1963 and has gone through six revisions. Its recent revitalization has been done under the influence of the model Peking opera. The character of Chun-hsiu has been moved to the principal position and the other positive characters, such as Wang, are given more weight, while the negative character, Pan, is made to look less comically assertive and more desperately foolish. Yet the opera's theme of a conservative manager, the setting in commerce, the set of the glossy neon-lit shop, the urban background and its acting style are reminiscent of the realist works of the fifties, influenced by the Russians. The comedy of character, especially the fun made of the blundering manager, was much appreciated by the local audience at the East Is Red Theatre, who also relished the many plays on words which put dialect to good use.

Hsiangyang Store appeared at the North China Drama Festival, held in Peking from 23 January to 18 February 1974. Other local operas at the festival were hailed as 'fruits of the cultural revolution.' Shansi province brought a Shantung *pangtzu* opera, *Ever Faster the Racing Horse*, set in the period of the cooperatives, and a *meiyun* opera, *Red Hearts Open to the Sun*, besides the ill-fated Shansi *pangtzu*, *Three Ascents of Peach Mountain*, by the province's senior company. Tientsin provided a *pingchu*, *Pierce the Fog and Set Sail*, about a boat laden with logs for the great Hai River flood control scheme on the north China plain. The crew overcomes the counter-revolutionary sabotage of one of their members en route. A *yin tiao* opera from Tangshan city called *Swallows Braving the Storm*, based on shadow plays, dealt with flood control in a mountain area. A Hopei *pangtzu*, *A Spring Swallow on Cloud Ridge*, told how a young 'barefoot' doctor, while administering medicine to the poor peasants, uncovers a quack.

A number of non-model Peking operas were shown by regional troupes. The Tientsin Peking Opera Company showed *Reed Marshes* about a guerrilla unit during the anti-Japanese war. The Lanfang Peking Opera Company's *Spring Swallows Spreading Their Wings* showed the maturing of educated youth who had settled in the countryside. The Peking Opera Company of the Inner Mongolian

Autonomous Region showed *Sons and Daughters on the Grasslands*, a revised version of an opera by the same company praised by Chiang Ch'ing in her 1964 speech, on which the puppet play *Red Flowers on the Grasslands* — also shown at the festival — was based.

A feature of the festival was the revival of comic short opera forms. Shansi brought a *puchu*, *Looking after Melons*. Tientsin Hopei Pangtzu Company had a triple bill of *Letting Someone Else Have the New Room*, *The Ferry* and *Communications Post in the Mountains*. Another triple bill was played by three companies. Hopei's Nanho County Yuchu Company gave performances of *Drawing the Line*, a thirty-minute comedy about a middle-aged peasant couple who hear that a channel of the Hai Ho Scheme is to be dug right through their living room. The wife does not want to leave her nice traditional-style house with a courtyard for a new brick house in a row. Her husband rebukes her: 'We should stand higher and have a wider view.' He points out that the tape-measure will divide selfishness from selflessness and the line it will draw is also the line between bourgeois and socialist thinking, the capitalist road and the socialist road. She decides to stay with relatives until after the autumn harvest when her new house will be ready.

The second opera, in *ssu hsien* style, was *Hammering the Iron*, a brilliantly executed comedy from Shihchiachuang city. A young couple argue over whether to make small farm tools on their home anvil for their own production team or for others and what sort of tools to make. The comic duet is built around the beats of the hammer on the iron. The husband at one point asks whether the wife knows *Song of the Dragon River*. Yes, she replies, she can sing some of it. Well, says the husband, why don't we solve the problem as Chiang Shui-ying (the heroine of the opera) did, by looking at the thing as a whole? She ends by agreeing to hammer iron for other teams and the hammering duet rises in a final crescendo.

The third opera, *All Thoughts Turned towards the Hai Ho*, a *luchu* opera by Linhsi County Cultural Troupe, Hopei, had three characters, a peasant, his wife and their grown-up daughter. The peasant and the daughter want to go and help on the flood control construction site but the wife wants to stay at home to look after her sister who is expecting a baby. The songs are rhymed for comic effect but the piece lacks the finer comedy of the first opera and the robust humour of the second. All three, however, were full of human character, the gestures, mime and movements were graceful yet not lacking in power, and the division between song and dialogue was less acute than in the model Peking operas. There was an effect of a continuous flow of movement and sound rather than a series of jagged patterns.

Apart from showing the success of applying model principles to local operas without a loss of local flavour, the North China Drama Festival had two interesting features. First, common to all new operas, was the existence of a 'bad element' in each play. Different from the merely erring character, such as the women in the three plays just discussed, whose political consciousness is low but who are nevertheless certainly not in antagonistic contradiction to the people, the 'bad element' is incorrigible, represents antagonistic forces, and has to be exposed by the end of the play. He is not even an enemy within the Party or, indeed, in the ranks of the masses at all. He is a left-over from the past who hides among the masses without really belonging to them and who may influence both masses and Party members until they see through him. He is always a man. The second notable feature was the predominantly rural setting of the plays. Within that setting was the recurring theme of water control and land reclamation, the two keys to China's self-sufficiency in grain production.

One of the festival's two major *huachu* also reflected rural themes. *On the Banks of Wild Horse River*, set in 1969 after a flood, describes how peasants of a remote mountain production brigade carve a canal along a precipitous route to tame a turbulent river and bring water to irrigate their land, unmasking class enemies as they go. Acted with a vigorous realism influenced by Peking opera gestures and poses, the play is a song in praise of collective effort in solving basic agricultural problems. The heroine, young Party branch secretary Kao Yen-hung, is played by twenty-five-year-old Chao Shu-chun, formerly an amateur actress, who in real life is known as 'a commune member outstanding for both ideology and work.'[51] In fact the fifty members of the Weichang County Cultural Troupe, set up in 1969, were drawn mainly from among young people in local factories and communes. The troupe's writing team, led by twenty-six-year-old Fan Ping, based their story on a real incident in a nearby county when a village Party secretary had risked his life igniting an explosive to clear a tunnel while building an irrigation network. 'It was the masses who created this play by their heroism,' Fan said.[52] The script was complete by 1971 and the play was performed 200 times in neighbouring villages in the next three years, being revised twenty-two times after criticism by the peasants.

A *huachu* with a very different setting, *In the Bloom of Youth* by the Tientsin Modern Drama Company, had a history of four years of revision before emerging at the festival. The play opens in the teachers' office of a small middle school on the outskirts of a seaside town. The time is 1963, before the cultural revolution but one year after Mao had warned 'Never forget class struggle.' Chang Hung, the daughter of a miner killed in a pit explosion before liberation, is fresh from college. She comes to teach at the school but soon finds herself up against the headmaster, Ho Hsiang, a teacher in an authoritarian mould. Ho wants his pupils to shut themselves up in their classrooms, memorize their texts, compete for marks in examinations and study to get a higher-paid job after leaving school.

Chang makes an issue of the head's attitude to two pupils, the son and daughter of a local fisherman. The daughter is compliant and studious. Delightedly, the head urges her to write an article for the local newspaper and make her name. Her brother, on the other hand, is a brawny, genial character who calls his sister a bookworm. He despises examinations as a left-over from the competitive past, loves to do manual work, relates his study to practice and has a good understanding of life. When he fails to turn up for an examination the head attempts to expel him from the school, telling the boy severely 'You were not born to study.' Rejecting the theory of innate ability, Chang Hung accuses the head of promoting intellectual education and neglecting moral and physical education, pointing out that his attitude favours pupils from bourgeois backgrounds. Visiting the boy's family she discovers that far from playing truant he had been rescuing a child from injury by a cart when he should have been at the examination. She learns that the daughter, though good at study, is selfish at home and never helps about the house, unlike the boy who is always doing odd jobs for other people. Furthermore, the pupils' father reveals that the school was built before liberation by a fish merchant out of the profits made from the fishermen's labour but that the school had then been reserved for children of the rich. 'Should the head, under a new guise, again be trying to deny the fisher youth the right to education?' asks the father.

Chang Hung asks the father to come to the school and give a talk about the school's history as a lesson in class education. But the head opposes the idea and with the agreement of higher authority in the Education Bureau he arranges Chang's transfer to another school. Meanwhile Chang fixes up a meeting of pupils and sympathetic teachers to criticize the head and the play ends with her ringing the school bell calling them to the meeting. Though she has to leave the school, the struggle continues.

The names of the play's characters define their level of consciousness. Ho Hsiang, literally translated, means 'How to soar.' Chin-jung, the daughter, means 'Prosperity and Fame.' Chen-kuang, the son, means 'Morning Light'. Chang Hung, meaning 'Always a Rainbow', implies bright and far-reaching persistence.

Obviously intended originally as a portrayal of a fore-runner of cultural revolution activists, Chang Hung is a thorn in the conservatives' flesh who uses arguments that were more relevant to the critical upsurge in progress in 1973—74. Then the role of examinations, the propriety of expelling backward students, and the practice of studying for marks and for a good job were again being called into question in China's schools and universities. It seems that as the play was revised Chang Hung came to stand as a representative of a radical who in the more conservative post-cultural revolution years was prepared 'to go against the tide'. The revision had not been easy. The company even abandoned performing the play in 1972 when, though workers in the main had welcomed it, 'others' had said the play 'disturbed the normal order of teaching' and 'went against' the raising of standards. *In the Bloom of Youth* played its part at the festival in renewing the claims of the cultural revolution and the company itself regarded their play as 'a counter-attack on the revisionist line in education.'[53]

The Peking Modern Drama Company's offering at the festival, a programme of three one-act plays, was more conservative. The first, *Chiao Chia Mountain*, was set beside a small rural power station which two 'educated youths', a brother and sister, had been assigned to look after. The boy worships science and wants to go to university to raise his standard. He thinks it is a waste of his time to settle in the countryside, a notion strengthened by the station's technician. When the village Party secretary, an old peasant, finds a nail driven into one of the station's water pipes, the boy is suspected of sabotage;

but it turns out the technician was the culprit. The second, *Up to Standard*, concerns the sale of a defective blouse when 'two attitudes to one defect' emerge. A shop assistant wants to change the blouse for a new one but the girl inspector, a cadre from the mill which manufactured the blouse, tells the customer not to be so fussy. Yet when she herself is given a blouse by her boyfriend, she strongly objects to a slight defect in it and demands he take it back to the shop. The theme of double standards is thus mingled with that of raising standards. The first customer turns out to have been the director of a textile mill in the north-east and a relative of the girl. The director reprimands the girl for 'bad thinking' and she criticizes herself. The comedy revolves not only around the blouse but around the boy-girl relationship, one selfless, the other selfish, and the unexpected appearance of the director/relative. In neither of these forty-five-minute plays, produced at the East Is Red Theatre, was there any lighting change. The third, *Before the Dynamiting*, was a discussion of plans to open up a mine on commune land, the hesitation over using dynamite so near to a reservoir and peasants' houses, and the justification for taking land out of arable use for mining purposes.

Of the three plays the audience appreciated best the urban comedy of *Up to Standard*. This play belongs to a *genre* common in the years of 'Liu Shao-chi's line'. The character of the genial and just director, the setting of the play in a city cadre's family, the boy-girl relationship, the theme of production (rather than political) problems, the concept of class struggle not as overthrow of the higher authority by the lower but as the remoulding of the lower by the higher, and the sophisticated use of slang in urban comedy were all familiar in the earlier period. The three plays in general supported the line of the current Five Year Plan for the modernization of China's economy, but behind all of them lay a concern for standards more in keeping with the orthodox professionalism admired before the cultural revolution.

Other one-act plays have followed a similar 'remoulding only' path. *Storm Warning*, which made up a triple bill with *The New Manager* and *An Extra Lesson* in a programme by the Central Broadcasting Cultural Troupe, is an exciting and humorous story of how a weather station struggles to give a correct forecast when a storm threatens a helicopter which is carrying a doctor to an injured militia leader. The play contains no explicit class struggle. The conflict is interiorized, psychological. The story involves a remoulding of the outlook of a wayward meteorologist, a girl — evidently the author herself, Kao Hung — who at first prefers learning her job from erudite books and despises the wise weather lore of the local old peasants. She is won over only by the successful application by her comrades of the contrary method of using both sources of knowledge.

The *hsiang sheng*, *The Telephone Line Is Always Open*, a cross-talk by two *chuyi* artists of the Cultural Troupe of the Political Department of the Navy, is a twenty-minute comic narration that again reflects the 'remoulding' idea. A fat man asks stupid questions of a thin man, who gives clever answers. Meeting in the street, the fat one asks, 'What's your job?' The thin one answers, 'I see few people but I talk a lot. My post is low but I can speak to any leader in the land.' The other doesn't guess, of course, that he's a people's telephone operator. 'I sit in my room and my voice reaches all over the country.' 'You have to have,' he says, 'a good relationship with callers to do your job well,' and he suggests the fat one has a try. He does so, but quickly runs out of patience, and in a witty mime accompanying comic rhymes he savages the air with a stabbing finger as, with increasing exasperation, he puts the plugs in the wrong sockets. 'Well? What's your answer?' asks the thin one. 'Scrap the telephone,' says the fat one. Reprimanding his friend for facetiousness, the thin one tells him the excitements of doing the job well. 'For example, I can make the telephone run after people.' — 'Oh? How?' — 'When someone's left his office to see a comrade, I can ring every office until I find the one he's in. Even when there's no line I can still get through.' — 'Really?' — 'Yes, I run there and take the message by hand. It's more video than videophone. We can even shake hands.' The fat one eventually concedes that you have to be conscientious if you want to serve the people.

Shanghai theatres have seen a similar emergence of 'remoulding' as a major theme. While the city's opera companies play the model operas and the local variants of them and while the Shanghai Dance Drama Company repeats the model ballets, the Shanghai People's Pingtan Company has produced a *pingtan* opera *On the Frontline in the Prevention of Schistosomiasis.* The opera advertizes Mao's cultural revolution instruction that in medical work stress should be put on the rural areas, but in choosing the subject of the campaign against snail fever the opera reminds people that the first successes in eradicating this disease of the paddy fields were in the 1950s, under the 'revisionist' medical line when undue stress was supposed to have been put on the cities. The opera is also another example of the 'raising standards' argument. The Shaohsing comic one-act opera *Half a Basket of Peanuts* tells how a peasant mother is 'remoulded' by her husband and son, who persuade her to 'stand higher' and 'see further' and not to keep the peanuts gleaned from the collective field for her own family.

Shanghai *huachu* has included *The Current of Steel*, about the determination of steel workers to produce the high quality steel needed for China's modernization rather than resort to importing it as the revisionists were said to have done. *Second Spring* deals with the struggle between the two lines in building up China's growing navy. The Shanghai Modern Drama Company's *Battle in the Shipyards* reflects a similar struggle for self-reliance in building 10,000 ton merchant ships, and makes the point that there is still a two-line struggle in the shipyard's present leadership over the issue of importing either entire ships or parts for constructing their own. The 'remoulding' line is reflected in the advice which the hero, Lei Hai-sheng, gives to angry workers who want to dismiss the conservative vice-chairman of the shipyard's revolutionary committee, 'No, we can't make him step aside, we must make him step forward.'

Shanghai took *Battle in the Shipyards* to a second festival, held in Peking in August and September 1974, a follow-up to the North China Drama Festival. The seventeen programmes shown there reviewed the progress of companies from Shanghai and Hunan in east-central China, Liaoning in the north-east and Kwangsi in the south-west. A significant feature of the festival was the experimental performance by the Shanghai Peking Opera Company of three new works which appear to be attempts to extend the boundaries of Peking opera. The most conventional of the three, *Boulder Bay*, is a contemporary story of village militia and fishermen unmasking Kuomintang agents who land on the south-east China coast. *Struggle on the Stormy Sea*, a short dance drama with rather little singing but a great deal of opera-style acrobatics, excitingly depicts the rescue of some fishermen caught in a storm. This drama was declared to be 'unique in its assimilation of the acrobatic combat and dance art of the Peking opera.' The third, *Trial of a Chair*, in only one act, is a revised version of a pre-cultural revolution piece which chronicles the fight of commune members against an overthrown but recalcitrant landlord. A Kwangsi troupe showed another new Peking opera, *Spring in the Yao Mountains*, set just after liberation, when the P.L.A. was helping the local Yao minority people to mop up the Kuomintang remnants.

Other operas were a *huaku* adaptation of *Shachiapang*, excerpts from *Fighting on the Plains* in the *chuangchu* opera, a form belonging to the Chuang minority, and scenes from models in seven other local opera styles. *Huachu* was represented by *Maple Bay* by a Hunan troupe, about peasant militia in the late 1920s; *Enthusiasm Seethes in the Mountains* by a Liaoning troupe, describing how miners quickly restore production in a ruined mine in the early days after liberation; and *Young Vanguard* by a Shanghai troupe, on a similar theme to *In the Bloom of Youth* but seen from a girl pupil's point of view.

The two 1974 festivals were followed by four further festivals in the capital in 1975, completing a major review of the work of companies from all the twenty-nine provinces, municipalities and autonomous regions of China. The entire series of six festivals saw the staging of forty-eight local operas adapted from the models, as well as over fifty original local operas and thirty-five new *huachu*. Over a thousand performances were given before audiences totalling nearly two million.

The festivals thus provided remarkable evidence of the scale of activity generated by the reforms which the cultural revolution introduced into opera and drama. That the reforms were not limited to these major theatrical forms but extended over the whole range of theatre arts was demonstrated in a yet further series of national festivals in 1975—76.

The National Puppet Theatre Festival in November and December 1975 introduced some sixty items, including adaptations of operas, dance dramas and children's stories, using rod, hand, string and shadow puppets, and presented by amateur and professional companies from fourteen provinces and cities.

At the National Dance Festival in January and February 1976, fifty-one companies put on 262 small-scale items (solos, *pas de deux* and *pas de trois*). Earlier dances, it was noted, had 'imitated the movements of storks and peacocks and were meaningless.' The new dances 'drew on the vocabulary of the ballet and Chinese folk-dances to portray today's heroes.'[54] Noteworthy were a number of items on industrial themes by worker amateurs. Also striking was the variety not only of dance styles but of character and setting: railwaymen on the track, soldiers on patrol, boat women on the Yangtze, a waitress in a restaurant, a miner at university, minority villagers in the mountains, women oil workers cleaning pipelines, an old couple bringing meals to a commune water-conservation building site.

The National Acrobatics Festival in the spring of 1976 presented a ten-week season comprising 440 items performed by thirty-two acrobatic companies. The mainly young acrobats, jugglers, conjurers and other artists eschewed hazardous stunts detrimental to their health and safety and developed new routines, including items of *wushu*, which displayed skill, vigour and vitality. Again, they borrowed from dance and opera to enlarge their vocabulary of gesture, mime and movement, as well as theme.

The National Festival of *Chuyi* in June 1976 showed 400 items in 182 *chuyi* styles. A further festival of *huachu* was scheduled for later in 1976.

During all these festivals, companies did not confine their performances to theatres but took them to workers' clubs in the Peking suburbs, railway yards, rural communes, mines, factories and army camps. A Shensi shadow puppet troupe went by bicycle. A Harbin puppet troupe put everything into two rubber-tyred carts to tour the communes. A Shantung *huachu* company took its own collapsible stage, its scenery, costumes and properties into the villages, all in one lorry. In a similar move away from theatre buildings, the national movement to repudiate Lin Piao and Confucius in 1974 encouraged major city companies to form special propaganda teams to tour the urban districts and perform agitational plays on mobile platforms and the backs of lorries.

The other big theatrical events of the year continued to be the festivities at the Spring Festival, May Day and National Day. The best of the items shown in Peking's parks on May Day 1974 were gathered into a programme at the Theatre of the Industrial Exhibition Hall which ran until the end of the month. The twelve pieces by eight groups indicate something of the range of popular entertainment and variety acts currently to be seen in the capital. Among the professional items, a mass choir of the Cultural Troupe of the General Political Department of the P.L.A. led off with a patriotic number, *It's Always Spring in Our Motherland*, followed by a song in praise of the anti-Lin and Confucius movement and an excerpt from *Shachiapang*. The team ended the show with a dance, *Fighting Horses*, showing the cavalry of the P.L.A. galloping in vigorous tests of strength and agility, accompanied by a big western-style orchestra in the pit. The orchestra of the Cultural Troupe of the Ministry of the Coal Industry, with a choir of forty, gave a recital of six songs in praise of Taching oil-workers. A girl from the Orchestra of the Central Newsreel and Documentary Film Studio gave a rendering of the traditional and very popular *Liuyang River* and a modern piece *Water Comes to Our Village*, both played on the *cheng*, an ancient zither-like instrument which has lately been modernized. A Uighur member of the P.L.A. troupe sang five songs from her home province of Sinkiang with great technical virtuosity and was much applauded. Two artists of the Cultural Troupe of the Navy's Political Department recited a *hsiang sheng*, *In Defence of Hsisha Island*, about the naval battle in January 1974 for some Chinese islands off Vietnam. The battle was the subject of many poems, ballads, songs and stories at the time. A clapper-ballad artist of the Peking Chuyi Company performed a fifteen-minute *kuai pan*, *Criticism Meeting by the Side of the Well*. His impersonations of contenders in a heated debate about Lin Piao and Confucius were received with much amusement and the audience was rewarded with two even more popular pieces, *Successors*, a very short dispute between parent and child, and *At a P.L.A. Camp*.

The show was completed by three amateur items: ten-year-old girls from the Chungshuhsie Primary School recited a *tan hsien* about a P.L.A. hero, Niu Wen-shu, who, at the price of his life, stopped an ex-landlord stealing green peppers from a commune field. Members of the Workers' Amateur Propaganda Team of the Coal-mining Bureau of Administration gave a powerful group recitation with stylized gestures and the workers' team of the Capital Iron and Steel Company performed their dance, *Flames of the Furnace Are Fiery*, accompanied by verses read over loudspeakers and a big western-style orchestra. The entire programme lasted nearly three hours, with an interval.

At the October 1974 celebrations of the twenty-fifth anniversary of the founding of the People's Republic, over eighty professional and amateur companies gave nearly 300 performances in Peking. Apart from the regular model works and the three new Peking operas from Shanghai, a Shantung company showed *Red Cloud Ridge*, a Peking opera version of *Ode to Yimeng*. Four new *huachu* were shown — *Battle Song over Cloud Spring* by the Peking Modern Drama Company, and a triple bill staged experimentally by the China Modern Drama Company, consisting of *Fighting Holidays*, *Frontline Position* and *Green Pine Ridge*.

The emergence of the China Modern Drama Company at these celebrations marked the full restoration of the *huachu* form to major status. This was confirmed a year later when Chen Chi-tung's ten-act *huachu*, *The Long March*, first performed in the late 1950s, was revived by the Modern Drama Company of the General Political Department of the P.L.A. on 1 October 1975 to mark the fortieth anniversary of that epic journey. The play had been revised by the company to stress the 'struggle between the two lines' of the time, and had been given 170 trial performances before worker-peasant-soldier audiences before its formal public re-opening. The National Festival of Modern Drama, promised for 1976, would further confirm the regained prestige of this form.

Reports of the May Day performances in 1976 mention the appearance of modern opera, by a China Modern Opera Company, suggesting a further extension of the adaptation of model works to another, perhaps new, form.[55]

The seventeen model works continued to play in Peking. Under the slogans 'Go to the great theatre of the countryside in the service of workers and peasants' and 'Deliver operas to the doorstep', the major Peking model companies went on a three-month tour of sixteen provinces in spring 1975. Other companies spent longer away: a troupe under the General Political Department of the P.L.A. spent six months on the Chinghai-Tibet plateau in 1974—75 and covered 4,000 kilometres to give 110 performances. Special praise was given to the hundreds of 'shoulder-pole art troupes' operating mainly at county level in the summer of 1975. The *People's Daily* urged theatre workers to learn from these 'knapsack, push-cart and shoulder-pole companies' and follow 'the shoulder-pole spirit.'[56]

A number of companies have toured abroad. Selections from traditional operas were taken to Paris in June 1955 by the old Peking Opera Company and later to other countries in the West, but, since the cultural revolution, and following the lead of the acrobats, tours have concentrated on countries of the Third World. The Peking Opera

Company of Peking visited Algeria in 1974. Art troupes and song and dance companies from Peking, Liaoning and the P.L.A. visited the Sudan, Trinidad and Tobago, Guyana, Venezuela, Korea, Albania, Yugoslavia, Romania and Pakistan in 1975—76. Their programmes of instrumental music, songs and dances were expertly played and invariably ended with renditions of some local numbers, much to the delight of their audiences. This is a custom that is reciprocated by foreign song and dance companies which have visited China from Korea, Vietnam, Albania and Pakistan.

The China Wushu Company visited five north African countries and Turkey, and took part in the independence celebrations in Mozambique, in 1975. At their performance in Britain the same year they were described by a London critic as 'a crack troupe with something beautiful to show.'[57]

In October—November 1975 acrobats from Tientsin toured Scandinavia. The Peking Opera Company of Shanghai spent fifty days in eight Japanese cities in summer 1976. Their twenty-four performances included *Taking Tiger Mountain by Strategy, Trial of a Chair* and *Chin Chiang Ferry*, and selections from *Boulder Bay*. Audiences in Japan were impressed by 'the great images of the Chinese people' to be found in these works.[58]

The pattern of professional productions seems to suggest that in reviving a great many theatrical forms which the drama workers have revolutionized under the influence of the model works, Chinese theatre has greatly enlarged its scope in expressing fundamental problems of her economic, social and political development. This has enriched her drama and made it more responsive to people's needs. At the same time such a great revival has set in motion certain contradictions. What has not been settled is the relationship between the models and the other works. The former by their authority dominate the latter but gradually the sheer quantity of the new material has begun to make itself felt. As it does, certain non-model features in it seem to provide something of a challenge to the models' predominance.

CHAPTER EIGHT

Conclusion. Trends for the Future

The revolutionary model Peking operas were officially acclaimed in 1974 as 'the embodiment of the correct approach to the national legacy.'[59] The concept of a play as providing a spiritual impetus to material change, a vehicle to propel history forward, is the essence of the agitational foundation upon which the efforts of the opera revolutionaries rest. Although their belief that they have succeeded with the model works in creating such vehicles may not be widely shared outside China, the dynamism of the revolutionaries' theoretical foundation is persuasive and of great importance for future developments in world theatre. It effectively removes the theatrical legacy from its status as a museum exhibit and places it in the front line of social activity.

Of course, the combination of revolutionary realism and revolutionary romanticism, a typification of the ideal, is not the only way that relations of revolutionary comradeship between proletarians may be shown on stage. Indeed, this is one of the points raised by critics within China who have denied Chu Lan's recent assertion that 'the fundamental task' of socialist literature and art is 'to portray typical proletarian heroes.'[60] The narrowness denoted by the word 'typical', these critics say, excludes a variety of dramatic methods that might be used with benefit by the proletariat.

The model works are certainly exclusive. With their emphasis on types, they have evolved a system of strict classification of characters, from the principal hero, through the grades of ordinary heroes, down to the most negative of the negative characters. It is natural that critics should refer to this tendency as stereotyping but defenders of the models have queried their motives: are they against stereotypes or against proletarian heroes? And they ask, pertinently, whether these critics ever protested that the emperors and scholars formerly occupying the stage were stereotypes. The renewed debate on the model operas at the time of the dismissal of Teng Hsiao-ping from his government posts in early 1976 made it clear that opposition to them remained at the highest level. Teng, it was said, regarded the emphasis placed on proletarian heroes as 'letting a single flower blossom'. He characterized the emphasis placed on class struggle in the model works as 'one-sided thinking in terms of absolutes'.[61]

With the removal of Chiang Ch'ing by the new Party leadership in October 1976 following the death of Mao, certain earlier works have been revived, such as the Peking opera version of *The White-haired Girl* which she was said to have criticized. More important, although her part in the revolutionizing of Peking opera has been revalued, the model works themselves have not yet been officially attacked. If anything they have been upgraded, since the accolade for their inspiration has been transferred from Chiang Ch'ing, who had previously claimed it, to Mao himself. Just before Teng Hsiao-ping's official reappearance in July 1977, however, the notion of 'the triple emphasis', contained in the model operas, was rejected.

As China moves, not out of capitalism, but out of feudalism, it is to be expected that her new culture will, in part, reflect modern equivalents of feudal hierarchical relations and these may, if only temporarily, mark the social relations depicted in her contemporary drama. The heroes the model works hold up as examples to the people are ideals such as are likely to be of use in a country that is emerging from feudalism into a type of democracy and from an agrarian into an industrial society and that is accumulating capital. A major shift in the locus of authority is taking place, particularly in the countryside. Where rural political authority used to be the landlord, it is now the Party secretary; clan authority is turning into the authority of the production brigade and the commune; religious authority finds its equivalent in the codes of conduct officials derive from Mao Tse-tung's writings. The model theatrical works are perhaps the most concentrated distillation in dramatic form of this new hierarchy.

The tension between two modes of organization of social relations — authoritarian hierarchy and democratic equality — lies at the heart of the major contradiction contained in the model drama. There is a deep discrepancy between the models' all-embracing authority and their agitational function. The model drama is at once an agent of the 'correct' and of rebellion. It embodies both an anaesthetizing and a disruptive purpose. So long as these two aspects maintain a unity of opposites, the models retain a certain usefulness, but one is sure to annihilate the other in the end. Either the models will ossify or they will fall apart. With the recent tendency towards a drama of 'remoulding', which, used in isolation, effectively precludes the concept of class struggle as armed overthrow, perhaps ossification is the more likely eventuality. Yet, if we are to believe Mao, that situation would only be temporary. New forms of rebel drama would arise to remove the dead hand of the new past. China's modern theatre will then move with her economy, her politics and her people on to the crest of the next wave.

Whatever the outcome of the present dispute, there is no doubt that drama as the political expression of groups of antagonistic publicists, each pursuing a certain class line, will be characteristic of Chinese theatre in the future, as it has been in the past. This is, objectively, not a feature of drama that is confined to China. But the form that this struggle takes in China, principled and intolerant, means that these groups will pursue mutually destructive courses, each claiming to act in the interests of the people. As these conflicts resolve themselves and the issues clarify along class lines, there will be periods when Chinese drama will move closer to mass popular involvement and periods when it will recede. The Chinese stage is a scene of contention and the protagonists are no less locked in battle now than they have been at any other time in the twenty-eight years since liberation.

References

Note — As regards the titles of contemporary plays and companies, the descriptions of performances, and the citing of figures, dates and places related to them, where no other reference is given it may be assumed the information derives from my own notes of performances I saw, or of talks I had with theatre workers in Peking, Tientsin, Wuhan, Sian and a number of communes and with teachers of Chinese Literature at Peking University, in 1965-67 and 1972-74.

1. 'Letter to the Yenan Peking Opera Troupe', 9 January 1944, in *Five Documents on Literature and Art*, Foreign Languages Press, Peking, 1967.
2. *Traditional Chinese Plays*, Vol. 1, University of Wisconsin Press, Madison, 1967, p. 15.
3. No. 1, 5 January 1973.
4. Interview with members of the staff of the Chinese Literature Department of Peking University, 6 July 1974.
5. Strong, Anna Louise, *China Fights for Freedom*, Lindsay Drummond, London, 1939, pp. 157-9.
6. Stein, Gunther, *The Challenge of Red China*, McGraw-Hill, New York, 1945, pp. 219-21.
7. Payne, Robert, *China Awake*, Dodd, Mead, New York, 1947, pp. 314-18.
8. Barrett, David D., *Dixie Mission: the United States Army Observer Group in Yenan, 1944,* University of California, Calif. 1970, pp. 51-2.
9. Payne, Robert, op. cit., p. 384.
10. Crook, Isabel and David, *The First Years of Yangyi Commune*, Routledge & Kegan Paul, London, 1966, pp. 267-72.
11. New China News Agency (NCNA) *Bulletin*, 14 March 1973.
12. No. 41, 1974, p. 22.
13. Speech to the 10th Plenary Session of the Eighth Central Committee, September 1962.
14. NCNA *Bulletin*, 18 March 1973.
15. Talks at the Yenan Forum on Art and Literature, May 1942.
16. *China Pictorial*, No. 3, 1973.
17. NCNA *Bulletin*, 27 December 1972, and *Chinese Literature*, No. 9, 1974, p. 100.
18. *Chinese Literature*, No. 1, 1974, p. 114.
19. *Chinese Literature*, No. 7, 1972, pp. 100-2.
20. Interview with members of the team, 26 December 1972.
21. *Chinese Literature*, No. 2, 1973, p. 93.
22. *Chinese Literature*, No. 8, 1973, p. 117.
23. *Chinese Literature*, No. 8, 1973, pp. 80-5.
24. 17 February 1974.
25. NCNA *Bulletin*, 24 May 1974; *Peking Review*, 2 August 1974, p. 19.
26. *The People's New Literature*, Cultural Press, Peking, 1950, p. 115.
27. 'Bright Future for Peking Opera' in *China in Transition* by Writers of *China Reconstructs*, Peking, 1957, pp. 346-50.
28. *Fanshen*, Vintage Books, New York, 1966, pp. 314-16.
29. Crook, Isabel and David, op. cit.
30. *China in Transition*, p. 356.

31. *Fifteen Strings of Cash*, Foreign Languages Press, Peking, 1957.
32. *Chinese Literature*, No. 3, 1971.
33. *A Great Revolution on the Cultural Front,* Foreign Languages Press, Peking, 1965.
34. *On the Revolution of Peking Opera*, Foreign Languages Press, Peking, 1968.
35. Ibid., pp. 17-19.
36. Ibid., pp. 20-3.
37. Ibid. pp. 28-32
38. Ibid. pp. 39-42; *China Reconstructs*, June 1973, p. 3; *Chinese Literature*, No. 8, 1970, p. 55.
39. Ibid., pp. 50-4.
40. Ibid., pp. 57-64.
41. *Chinese Literature*, No. 10, 1967, pp. 59-60.
42. Ansley, Clive, *The Heresy of Wu Han*, University of Toronto Press, Toronto, 1971.
43. Ibid., pp. 89-90.
44. *Summary of the Forum on Work in Literature and Art in the Armed Forces,* Foreign Languages Press, Peking, 1968.
45. *On Stanislavsky's 'System'*, Foreign Languages Press, Peking, 1969.
46. Hinton, William, 'Hundred Day War', *Monthly Review*, July-August 1972, pp. 134-6.
47. Interview with players, October 1966.
48. *Chinese Literature*, No. 10, 1967, p. 137.
49. Ansley, Clive, op. cit., p. 8.
50. *China Reconstructs*, February 1974, p. 15.
51. *China Reconstructs*, May 1974, p. 28; *Chinese Literature*, No. 5, 1974, pp. 109-11.
52. NCNA *Bulletin*, 1 March 1974.
53. *Kwangming Daily*, 17 February 1974.
54. *Peking Review,* No. 10, 5 March 1976.
55. NCNA *Bulletin*, 30 April 1976.
56. *People's Daily*, 11 June 1975.
57. Wardle, Irving, *The Times*, 21 May 1975.
58. NCNA *Bulletin*, 15 May 1976.
59. NCNA Special Issue, Hong Kong, 1 October 1974.
60. 'A Decade of Revolution in Peking Opera', *Peking Review*, No. 31, 2 August 1974.
61. NCNA *Bulletin*, 9 April 1976 and Chu Lan's 'Deepen the Criticism of Teng Hsiao-ping, Persevere in the Revolution in Literature and Art — Study "Talks at the Yenan Forum on Literature and Art" ', *People's Daily*, 23 May 1976.

Further Reading

Apart from works mentioned in the References, the following may be of interest to readers:

1. Alley, Rewi, *Peking Opera*, New World Press, Peking, 1957.
2. Chen, Jack, *The Chinese Theatre*, Dennis Dobson, London, 1949.
3. *Fifteen Strings of Cash, The Fisherman's Revenge, The Forsaken Wife, Love under the Willows, The Runaway Maid* (traditional Szechuan, Cantonese, *pingchu, kunchü* and Peking operas, revised) published individually, Foreign Languages Press, Peking, 1956-58.
4. Fokkema, D.W., *Literary Doctrine in China and Soviet Influence 1956-1960*, Mouton & Co., The Hague, 1965.
5. Gamble, Sydney D., *Chinese Village Plays*, Philo Press, Amsterdam, 1970.
6. Halson, Elizabeth, *Peking Opera: A Short Guide*, Oxford University Press, Hong Kong, 1966.
7. Hu Ko, *Locust Tree Village*, Foreign Languages Press, Peking, 1961.
8. Lau, Joseph S.M., *Tsao Yu*, Hong Kong University Press, Hong Kong, 1970.
9. Lin Mo-han, *Raise High the Banner of Mao Tse-tung's Thought on Art and Literature*, Foreign Languages Press, Peking, 1961.
10. Lu Ting-yi, *Let a Hundred Flowers Blossom, a Hundred Schools of Thought Contend*, Foreign Languages Press, Peking, 1964.
11. Mackerras, Colin P., *Amateur Theatre in China 1949-1966*, Australian National University Press, Canberra, 1973.
12. Mackerras, Colin P., *The Chinese Theatre in Modern Times: From 1840 to the Present Day*, Thames & Hudson, London, 1975.
13. Mackerras, Colin P., *The Rise of the Peking Opera 1770-1870*, Oxford University Press, London, 1972.
14. Obraztsov, Sergei, *The Chinese Puppet Theatre*, Faber & Faber, London, 1961.
15. *On the Docks, The Red Lantern, Shachiapang, Taking Tiger Mountain by Strategy, Song of the Dragon River* (Peking operas), *Red Detachment of Women* (ballet), published individually, Foreign Languages Press, Peking, 1971-73.
16. Scott, A.C., *The Classical Theatre of China*, Allen & Unwin, London, 1957.
17. Scott, A.C., *An Introduction to the Chinese Theatre*, Donald Moore, Singapore, 1958.
18. Scott, A.C., *Literature and the Arts in Twentieth Century China*, Anchor, New York, 1963.
19. Snow, Lois Wheeler, *China on Stage*, Random House, New York, 1972.
20. *To Find Men Truly Great and Noble-hearted We Must Look Here in the Present* — In Praise of the Modern Revolutionary Peking opera *Taking Tiger Mountain by Strategy*, Foreign Languages Press, Peking, 1971.
21. Ting Yi and Ho Ching-chih, *The White-haired Girl* (1953 version) in *Modern Drama from Communist China*. Also contains *Letters from the South*, Sun Yu's *The Women's Representative*, Lao Sheh's *Dragon Beard Ditch, The Red Lantern* (1965 version) and Kuan Han-ching's *Snow in Midsummer*, New York University Press and University of London Press, 1970.

22. *Traditional Chinese Plays* (Vol. 1, *Ssu Lang Visits His Mother*; *The Butterfly-Dream*. Vol. 2, *Longing for Worldly Pleasures*; *Fifteen Strings of Cash*). University of Wisconsin Press, Madison, 1967, 1969.
23. Tsao Yu, *Thunderstorm*, Foreign Languages Press, Peking, 1958.
24. Tsao Yu, *Sunrise*, Foreign Languages Press, Peking, 1960.
25. Tuan Cheng-pin and Tu Shih-tsun, *Taming the Dragon and the Tiger*, Foreign Languages Press, Peking, 1961.
26. Tung, Fu-ming, *The History of the Chinese Puppet and Shadow Plays*, China Institute of Music and Drama, Peking, 1937.
27. *War Drums on the Equator*, Foreign Languages Press, Peking, 1966.
28. Wimsatt, Genevieve, *Chinese Shadow Shows*, Harvard University Press, Mass., 1936.

General Index

Index of Works

List of Chinese Characters

Chen Kwei-chen	陈桂珍
Chen Li-ning	陈里宁
Chen Shu-fang	陈书舫
Chetzuhsi	折子戏
Chi Pen-yu	戚本禹
Chou Hsin-fang	周信芳
Chou Yang	周扬
Chuanchu	川剧
Chuangchu	壮剧
Chu Lan	初澜
Chuyi	曲艺
Erh-huang	二黄
Hao Jan	浩然
Hsiang sheng	相声
Hsia Yen	夏衍
Hsi-pi	西皮
Huachu	话剧
Huaku	花鼓
Huchu	沪剧
Ku Ko	胡可
Hung Chen	洪辰
Hung Hsien-nu	红线女
Kao Hung	高虹
Kao Yu-pao	高玉宝
Kao Tse-cheng	高则诚
Ko Ching-shih	柯庆施
Kuai pan	快板
Kuai shu	快书
Kuan Han-ching	关汉卿
Kunchü	昆曲
Lao Sheh	老舍
Li Chih-hua	李之华
Li Chun	李准
Lin Mo-han	林默涵
Luchu	鲁剧
Lu Hsun	鲁迅
Lu Ting-yi	陆定一
Ma Chien-ling	马乾麟
Mao Hui-fang	茅惠芳
Ma Tai	马泰
Mei Lan-fang	梅兰芳
Meiyun	梅韵
Pangtzu	梆子
Peking opera (*ching chu*)	京剧
Peng Chen	彭真
Peng Teh-huai	彭德怀
Piao yen chang	表演唱
Pingchu	评剧
Ping hua	评书
Pingtan	评弹
Puchu	蒲剧
Ssu hsien	丝弦
Tai Ai-lien	戴爱莲
Ta ku shu	大鼓
Tan hsien	单纮
Tan Hsin-pei	谭鑫培
Tan tzu	弹词
Tao Jan Ting	陶然亭
Tien Han	田汉
Ting Ling	丁玲
Tsa chu	什剧
Tsao Yu	曹禺
Tuan Cheng-pin	段承宾
Wang Chuan-sung	王崇生
Wang Kuo-fu	王国福
Wang Li	王力
Wang Shu-yuan	王叔元
Wuchu	吴剧
Wu Han	吴晗
Wushu	武术
Yangko	秧歌
Yao Wen-yuan	姚文元
Yin tiao	影调
Yuan Chang-ching	阮章竞
Yuehchu (Cantonese)	粤剧
Yuehchu (Shaohsing)	越剧
Yu Hui-yung	于会泳